T0209417

An Analysis of

Edmund Burke's

Reflections on the Revolution in France

Riley Quinn

Published by Macat International Ltd
24:13 Coda Centre, 189 Munster Road, London SW6 6AW.

Distributed exclusively by Routledge
2 Park Square, Milton Park, Abingdon, Oxon OX14 4RN
711 Third Avenue, New York, NY 10017, USA

Routledge is an imprint of the Taylor & Francis Group, an informa business

www.macat.com
info@macat.com

Cataloguing in Publication Data
A catalogue record for this book is available from the British Library.
Library of Congress Cataloguing-in-Publication Data is available upon request.
Cover illustration: Etienne Gilfillan

ISBN 978-1-912303-18-2 (hardback)
ISBN 978-1-912127-93-1 (paperback)
ISBN 978-1-912282-06-7 (e-book)

Notice
The information in this book is designed to orientate readers of the work under analysis,
to elucidate and contextualise its key ideas and themes, and to aid in the development
of critical thinking skills. It is not meant to be used, nor should it be used, as a
substitute for original thinking or in place of original writing or research. References and
notes are provided for informational purposes and their presence does not constitute
endorsement of the information or opinions therein. This book is presented solely for
educational purposes. It is sold on the understanding that the publisher is not engaged
to provide any scholarly advice. The publisher has made every effort to ensure that
this book is accurate and up-to-date, but makes no warranties or representations with
regard to the completeness or reliability of the information it contains. The information
and the opinions provided herein are not guaranteed or warranted to produce particular
results and may not be suitable for students of every ability. The publisher shall not be
liable for any loss, damage or disruption arising from any errors or omissions, or from
the use of this book, including, but not limited to, special, incidental, consequential or
other damages caused, or alleged to have been caused, directly or indirectly, by the
information contained within.

CONTENTS

THE MACAT LIBRARY

The Macat Library is a series of unique academic explorations of seminal works in the humanities and social sciences – books and papers that have had a significant and widely recognised impact on their disciplines. It has been created to serve as much more than just a summary of what lies between the covers of a great book. It illuminates and explores the influences on, ideas of, and impact of that book. Our goal is to offer a learning resource that encourages critical thinking and fosters a better, deeper understanding of important ideas.

Each publication is divided into three Sections: Influences, Ideas, and Impact. Each Section has four Modules. These explore every important facet of the work, and the responses to it.

This Section-Module structure makes a Macat Library book easy to use, but it has another important feature. Because each Macat book is written to the same format, it is possible (and encouraged!) to cross-reference multiple Macat books along the same lines of inquiry or research. This allows the reader to open up interesting interdisciplinary pathways.

To further aid your reading, lists of glossary terms and people mentioned are included at the end of this book (these are indicated by an asterisk [*] throughout) – as well as a list of works cited.

Macat has worked with the University of Cambridge to identify the elements of critical thinking and understand the ways in which six different skills combine to enable effective thinking.
Three allow us to fully understand a problem; three more give us the tools to solve it. Together, these six skills make up the **PACIER** model of critical thinking. They are:

ANALYSIS – understanding how an argument is built
EVALUATION – exploring the strengths and weaknesses of an argument
INTERPRETATION – understanding issues of meaning

CREATIVE THINKING – coming up with new ideas and fresh connections
PROBLEM-SOLVING – producing strong solutions
REASONING – creating strong arguments

To find out more, visit **WWW.MACAT.COM.**

CRITICAL THINKING AND *REFLECTIONS ON THE REVOLUTION IN FRANCE*

Primary critical thinking skill: REASONING
Secondary critical thinking skill: ANALYSIS

Edmund Burke's 1791 *Reflections on the Revolution in France* is a strong example of how the thinking skills of analysis and reasoning can support even the most rhetorical of arguments. Often cited as the foundational work of modern conservative political thought, Burke's *Reflections* is a sustained argument against the French Revolution. Though Burke is in many ways not interested in rational close analysis of the arguments in favour of the revolution, he points out a crucial flaw in revolutionary thought, upon which he builds his argument. For Burke, that flaw was the sheer threat that revolution poses to life, property and society.

Sceptical about the utopian urge to utterly reconstruct society in line with rational principles, Burke argued strongly for conservative progress: a continual slow refinement of government and political theory, which could move forward without completely overturning the old structures of state and society. Old state institutions, he reasoned, might not be perfect, but they work well enough to keep things ticking along. Any change made to improve them, therefore, should be slow, not revolutionary.

While Burke's arguments are deliberately not reasoned in the 'rational' style of those who supported the revolution, they show persuasive reasoning at its very best.

ABOUT THE AUTHOR OF THE ORIGINAL WORK

Born in Ireland in 1729, **Edmund Burke**'s initial studies were in law, but he found himself drawn first to writing, then politics. He entered the British parliament in 1765 and soon won a reputation for his debating skills and strong political convictions, including views on the American and French Revolutions and British imperial practices in India. Burke died in 1797, and has since come to be regarded as the father of modern English conservatism.

ABOUT THE AUTHOR OF THE ANALYSIS

Riley Quinn holds master's degrees in politics and international relations from both LSE and the University of Oxford.

ABOUT MACAT

GREAT WORKS FOR CRITICAL THINKING

Macat is focused on making the ideas of the world's great thinkers accessible and comprehensible to everybody, everywhere, in ways that promote the development of enhanced critical thinking skills.

It works with leading academics from the world's top universities to produce new analyses that focus on the ideas and the impact of the most influential works ever written across a wide variety of academic disciplines. Each of the works that sit at the heart of its growing library is an enduring example of great thinking. But by setting them in context – and looking at the influences that shaped their authors, as well as the responses they provoked – Macat encourages readers to look at these classics and game-changers with fresh eyes. Readers learn to think, engage and challenge their ideas, rather than simply accepting them.

'Macat offers an amazing first-of-its-kind tool for interdisciplinary learning and research. Its focus on works that transformed their disciplines and its rigorous approach, drawing on the world's leading experts and educational institutions, opens up a world-class education to anyone.'

Andreas Schleicher
Director for Education and Skills, Organisation for Economic Co-operation and Development

'Macat is taking on some of the major challenges in university education … They have drawn together a strong team of active academics who are producing teaching materials that are novel in the breadth of their approach.'

Prof Lord Broers,
former Vice-Chancellor of the University of Cambridge

'The Macat vision is exceptionally exciting. It focuses upon new modes of learning which analyse and explain seminal texts which have profoundly influenced world thinking and so social and economic development. It promotes the kind of critical thinking which is essential for any society and economy. This is the learning of the future.'

Rt Hon Charles Clarke, former UK Secretary of State for Education

'The Macat analyses provide immediate access to the critical conversation surrounding the books that have shaped their respective discipline, which will make them an invaluable resource to all of those, students and teachers, working in the field.'

Professor William Tronzo, University of California at San Diego

WAYS IN TO THE TEXT

KEY POINTS

- The politician and political thinker Edmund Burke was born in Ireland—then a part of the United Kingdom—in 1729 and died in England in 1797.

- Written in 1790, *Reflections on the Revolution in France* is Burke's response to the French Revolution* of 1789. Here, he outlines the danger of radicalism,* arguing that tradition is valuable and political change should be both gradual and carefully handled.

- *Reflections* is one of the founding works of modern conservative* thought.

Who Was Edmund Burke?

Edmund Burke was born in Dublin, Ireland in 1729 when the country was still part of the United Kingdom. His mother was Roman Catholic* and his father was Church of Ireland,* or Protestant.* He had a middle-class upbringing because his father was a solicitor, studied at a Quaker* school, and went on to Trinity College Dublin. After graduating in 1750, Burke moved to England to study law. However, law did not satisfy him and he turned first to writing, then to politics. His political career began in 1765 when he became private secretary to Lord Rockingham,* then the leader of the Whig Party.*

Rockingham sponsored Burke to become a Member of Parliament*
for the Whig Party, which later became the Liberal Party.*

Burke's rise to social prominence and political power was very
unusual. He was an Irishman of relatively humble origins, but after
joining the Whigs he moved in the same circles as landed aristocracy,*
the social class that owns land and property that generates income for
the owner without the owner doing the work. From the start of his
political career Burke was closely involved in all the debates of the day.
He was in favor of introducing limits to the power of the king and
accepted the grievances of the American Colonies, fighting hard
against Britain going to war with America over independence in 1775.
Burke wrote well-received pamphlets outlining his views on both of
these issues. In 1789, the French aristocrat Charles-Jean-François
Depont* asked Burke what he thought of the French Revolution and
Burke decided to reply publically, writing *Reflections on the Revolution
in France*. It quickly became a bestseller and helped to establish Burke
as one of the major political thinkers of his time. He died in
Beaconsfield, England in 1797 at the age of 68. But his ideas have
remained influential to this day.

What Does *Reflections on the Revolution in France* Say?

Edmund Burke felt the radical ideas that had inspired the French
Revolution were both seductive and dangerous, and that Britain
needed to be protected from them. He wrote *Reflections on the
Revolution in France* as a way of stopping this movement from spreading
across the English Channel to Britain. The book sets out his "counter-
theory." Burke recognized, for example, that the idea that "the people"
deserved to rule their countries was a very attractive one that could
easily take hold in Britain. There were many people in British public
life who saw the French Revolution as the dawn of an exciting new
era and who wanted similar reforms. These people included a faction
of his own political party, the Whigs. They believed the principle that

"the people" should rule applied to Britain as much as it did to France. They also thought England's own revolution—the Glorious Revolution* of 1688, when the Roman Catholic King James II* was overthrown and a system where the monarch does not have absolute power was introduced—already proved "the people" should have the same rights. In *Reflections* Burke says legitimate political change needs to come gradually and not through revolution. He thinks that radical beliefs, no matter how rational they might seem, will cause society to disintegrate.

One of the most important ideas Burke opposes is that abstract principles—ideas that people had thought up—can form the basis of a society. He believes society is too complex and too important to be shaped by ideas alone. To him, society is a kind of inheritance. Social institutions are shaped by successive generations slowly finding out exactly what works. For example, England has a king because England has always had a king, and having a king has always kept English society working. If the way the country operated needs reform, then reform should happen slowly so what is clearly already working can be preserved. In Burke's view, governments that are invented and reinvented based on what is intellectually fashionable at a particular time will descend into chaos.

Burke believed the three guiding principles for society were "prejudice," "presumption," and "prescription." "Prejudice" means that people stick to their own beliefs without needing to establish them as fact. So, for example, in a Roman Catholic country the people will be inclined to think that Catholicism works better than other systems of belief; they will be predisposed towards Catholicism. "Presumption" means that people assume that what has worked in the past, and what works now, will work in the future. So, the people of a Roman Catholic country assume that Catholicism will continue to be the best system. "Prescription" means that institutions such as the Catholic Church are only obeyed because they demand obedience. So citizens believe in Catholicism because they are told to. In Burke's view it was these three principles that made governments unique to the people they govern.

In *Reflections* Burke speaks out against the idea of a perfect state, or utopia.* Instead of overthrowing an existing system in search of utopia, he says, it is better to keep adjusting our existing political systems until we find the perfect one. *Reflections* argues that politics is always more about pure logic than it is about noble ideas. Burke reminds politicians that radical change inspired by noble ideas can have unintended—and horrific—consequences. In doing this Burke correctly predicted The Terror*—the time of extreme political violence between 1792 and 1794 that followed the French Revolution. During The Terror there were mass, and often highly subjective, executions of those seen as "enemies of the Revolution."

To Burke, fending off the ideas of the French Revolution was a burning issue and he did not want to look at the argument from both sides. *Reflections* is a book with a political purpose, a piece of propaganda, as much as it is a political theory text.

Why Does *Reflections on the Revolution in France* Matter?

The French Revolution was a turning point in European history because it spread hope for freedom, but also the fear of violence everywhere. Published in 1790 in the midst of the Revolution, *Reflections* was both a bestseller and a major political text—and it still carries weight today. Burke explores the British political debate about the French Revolution of the time, but he also looks at government reform in general, which means there is plenty of material that is of lasting value for people interested in politics and history.

Burke's rejection of the idea that radical thinking leads to a better system has led to him being seen as a founding father of modern conservatism. *Reflections* is hailed by some as a kind of "conservative manifesto." Burke has been an inspiration to many leading conservative thinkers, including nineteenth-century British journalist Walter Bagehot* and Prime Minister Benjamin Disraeli,* American political theorist Russell Kirk,* and the contemporary cultural commentator David Brooks.*

Reflections helps to build a framework that can be used to evaluate political reform projects. Burke asks the key question that can be applied to political reform in any historical or political context: "Is this sensible change?" By sensible Burke means, "Is this a change that will preserve what worked, however imperfectly, about the old ways?"

Burke's views are valued by modern conservatives in the United States. Russell Kirk said that Reflections was the first work of "conscious conservatism"[1] as it explained the importance of looking at society as needing to be nurtured, not cut down and replaced with something entirely new. This had been an important part of the debate about systems of government when the old ways of the United States and the new system of the Soviet Union* battled it out for ideological supremacy during The Cold War* between 1947 and 1989.

There has also been discussion about how Burke's views have been interpreted by US conservatives in more recent times, especially in relation to American foreign policy in the Middle East. David Brooks has argued that the US government of George W. Bush,* while seeing itself as conservative, did not follow Burke's principals in its policies in invading Afghanistan and Iraq following the terrorist attacks on New York in 2001.* The administration believed that by changing political institutions in these countries, society there would improve. Brooks believes they missed the point, because Burke said society does not benefit from wholesale change, only gradual changes.

The tone of Burke's rejection of liberal* politics—those founded on ideas of individual freedom and liberty—borders on the furious, and many modern readers reject him for his angry language. To get the most from reading Burke's *Reflections* the reader needs to look beyond the passionate prose that is designed to convince, and understand that his argument is not anti-liberal, it is pro-pragmatic.* Burke wants politics to be based on practical, sensible practices, not theoretical ideas.

NOTES

1   Russell Kirk, *The Conservative Mind: Burke to Eliot* (Washington, D.C.: Eagle Publishing, 2001), 6.

SECTION 1
INFLUENCES

THE AUTHOR AND THE HISTORICAL CONTEXT

KEY POINTS

- *Reflections on the Revolution in France* was part of a debate between "radicals"* and "conservatives"* that has helped form modern ideas of what politics should be.

- Edmund Burke was born into a middle-class Irish family and worked his way into Parliament* as a member of the Whig* Party.

- Burke wrote *Reflections* as a response to the ideas that underpinned the French Revolution* and to defend Britain from their influence.

Why Read This Text?

Edmund Burke's *Reflections on the Revolution in France* is widely considered one of the most important and influential works of Western political conservatism. Burke's main concern is to defend the ways of the ancien régime*—the social and political system that ruled France from the fifteenth century until the late eighteenth century—in the face of radical change. But more importantly than that he wanted to prevent Britain from being seduced by radical French ideology.* Burke wanted to discredit the ideas of the revolutionaries and reformers of the French Revolution who he felt wanted a government system based on theories and ideas. To Burke, politics was much more based on experience than ideas. Burke felt that political questions could only be answered by looking at how governments actually deliver order and safety and not by imagining what an ideal government would look like. It is this insight that makes *Reflections*

> ❝ In [Burke's] *Reflections* we confront a public political actor of fundamentally liberal values forced by rapidly unfolding events to reconsider his understanding of the preconditions of political liberty. Burke was a liberal carrying out that difficult, self-imposed assignment determined that no one resist his questions, ignore his arguments or evade his conclusions. ❞
>
> Frank M. Turner, "The Political Actor Thinking," Introduction to *Reflections*

more than an anti-revolutionary work and what has turned it into a template for modern conservatism.

Author's Life

Edmund Burke was born into a middle-class family in Dublin, Ireland in 1729. He was educated at a Quaker* school and went on to study at Trinity College, Dublin. Burke moved to England in 1750 to follow a legal career, but he left the world of law quite quickly to begin a new career first in writing, then in politics. He joined the Whig Party which eventually became the Liberal Party* toward the end of the nineteenth century. The Whigs were in favor of individual liberty and "small" government—a government that sets low taxes and limits its own activities and powers. Burke first entered Parliament as private secretary to Charles Watson-Wentworth, 2nd Marquess of Rockingham*. Rockingham was the Chairman of the Whig Party and he sponsored Burke to become a Member of Parliament himself. Burke was an outsider in English political life, a middle-class Irishman whose social advancement had been enabled and was supported by members of the aristocracy*—the upper class comprising those of noble birth with hereditary titles. It is possible that the ideas of the French Revolution of 1789—which included overthrowing the aristocracy—may have felt like a personal threat to him.

According to Frank M. Turner,* Burke saw the ideas behind the French Revolution as a "deadly radicalism that has hijacked the vocabulary of political liberty."[1] He wrote *Reflections* as a warning against these ideas, to set himself up in opposition to the dangers of radicalism in general and to defend the British monarchy.* His ideas touched a chord with people in Britain and *Reflections* became a bestseller. However, the book caused a major split in his party because many Whigs were actually in favor of the French Revolution, in particular those who supported Charles James Fox* to succeed Lord Rockingham in the Whig Party. Despite this, *Reflections* helped to establish Burke as one of the major political thinkers of his era and he continued to be so right up until his death at the age of 68 in 1797.

Author's Background

Burke was active in politics at a dramatic time of important historical events, such as the beginning of the Industrial Revolution* in Britain (around 1760) and the American War of Independence (1775–83). But the French Revolution of 1789 is widely seen as the most important event of Burke's era, an event that changed the course of modern history. France was both an absolute monarchy (a country ruled by a king who has unrestricted power over his subjects) and a theocracy* (a society where the clergy are officially recognized as rulers in the name of God). It was also a nation that was extraordinarily rigid at a social level. Members of the higher social orders believed their privileged position was natural and unchangeable. It is highly unlikely that a middle-class thinker such as Burke, who became a well-respected politician in England, could have reached the same position in France. The American historian Sylvia Neely* wrote, "The society of the Ancien Régime was hierarchical, in an order believed to have been created by God. The king was at the apex, and below him were his subjects." The king's subjects were divided into three "estates": religious officials, aristocrats, and commoners. The commoners were known as the "Third Estate," and were the least powerful among them.[2] There was a widespread belief that the king, aristocrats, and clergy ruled because it was their *destiny* to rule, not because they had any proven ability to lead or to rule. This traditional French society was violently overthrown by radical reformers during the French Revolution.

The revolutionary "moment" came in May 1789 when representatives of the Third Estate declared that the existing government was illegitimate and that in fact they, the Third Estate, were now the government, which they called the National Assembly.* On July 14, 1789 the political battle turned violent when the common people stormed the Bastille—a royal prison in the French capital, Paris, where arms were stored and which was a symbol of the king's power. After this, the French state was rebuilt completely.

The French Revolution had many complex causes, and different thinkers tend to pick out different reasons as to why it happened. Prime among these are the following:

- new ideas—such as "popular sovereignty"* or the principle that the people have the right to rule
- new taxations—such as those introduced to help pay for France's role in the American War of Independence
- accidental circumstances—such as the successive failures of grain harvests which led to famine in the lower classes and deep resentment of those who could easily afford bread.

The fact that the Third Estate was socially marginalized and decided to revolt and demand equality with the other two estates certainly contributed to the French Revolution. French thinker and clergyman Abbé Sieyès* wrote: "What is the third estate? Everything. What has it been up to now in the political order? Nothing. What does it ask? To become something."[3] The American historian James R. Arnold* wrote: "The Third Estate asked to have as many representatives in [the government] as the other two estates combined."[4] This was a radical shift in favor of populism.

Burke feared these radical ideas would reach Britain and saw evidence that they were doing so. In 1789, the radical democrat* Thomas Paine* wrote a private letter to Burke. In it Paine said, "The Revolution in France is certainly a forerunner to other Revolutions in Europe."[5] This sense of the imminent threat of a revolution in Britain made Burke want to respond. He wrote *Reflections* mainly for his fellow politicians and to "alert the party leaders … to the dangers to which radical opinions, however innocent and however sincerely held, could run."[6]

NOTES

1   Frank M. Turner, "Edmund Burke: The Political Actor Thinking," Introduction to Edmund Burke, *Reflections on the Revolution in France*, ed. Frank M. Turner (New Haven, CT: Yale University Press, 2003), xiv.

2   Syliva Neely, *A Concise History of the French Revolution* (Lanham, MD: Rowman & Littlefield, 2008), 12.

3   Abbé Sieyès, quoted in James R. Arnold, *The Aftermath of the French Revolution* (Minneapolis, MN: Twenty First Century Books, 2009), 13.

4   Arnold, *Aftermath*, 13.

5   Frank O'Gorman, *Edmund Burke: His Political Philosophy* (London: George Allen & Unwin, 1973), 110.

6   O'Gorman, *Edmund Burke*, 109.

ACADEMIC CONTEXT

KEY POINTS

- Enlightenment* ideals, which underpin the ideas of the French Revolution,* were concerned with finding the roots of authority in universal ideas of human nature and ethics.
- Enlightenment philosophy was based on ideas about how society *should* be organized.
- Burke was part of the "Counter-Enlightenment"* and argued against defining politics based on attractive but theoretical ideas.

The Work in Its Context

Edmund Burke's *Reflections on the Revolution in France* is considered a founding work of conservatism,* but it cannot be pigeonholed into a single tradition. It is best understood now as part of the "Counter-Enlightenment." The Enlightenment was the name given to an intellectual movement in seventeenth- and eighteenth-century Europe where science asserted itself against tradition as the principal force for organizing society. "Tradition" can be thought of as doing things in a given way because that is how it has "always" been done. The Enlightenment tried to challenge traditional figures of authority such as the Church, the aristocracy, and the established institutions of state and government. Its tools were reason and analysis.

The British historian Norman Hampson* writes, "Looking back on the seventeenth century, one can notice the evolution of certain attitudes, especially the establishment of a verifiable 'science', then doubt and confusion eventually gave way to self-confidence, the belief that the unknown was merely the undiscovered."[1] There was great

> ❝ For Burke, there was often something hubristic*
> about those who would seek to step outside their
> received social contexts in an effort to find an objective
> ground for their values. ❞
>
> David Dwan and Christopher Insole, "Introduction: Philosophy in Action,"
> *The Cambridge Companion to Edmund Burke*

excitement at the time about applying the idea of science into all
realms of life, including politics.

Many people were starting to believe that anything unknown
could be discovered and that some things could be discovered to be
absolutely true.

Overview of the Field

Early political scientists, such as the seventeenth-century English
philosopher Thomas Hobbes,* tried to find a scientifically derived
theory of how political authority was instigated that had no basis in
tradition. That is to say, Hobbes saw man as nothing more than matter
and motion obeying the same physical laws as other matter and
motion. Hobbes used an intellectual idea called "the state of nature"*
to describe society along these scientific lines. The state of nature is an
imaginary environment before society formed where humanity lives
separately and then comes together to make up a political community.
In Hobbes's conception of the state of nature he believes that all men
are completely free. By this Hobbes means man is not bound by any
laws or forces other than those mankind can impose on each other. In
other words, I keep my own food, but you can make me give you my
food if you are strong enough to take it.

To Hobbes it is inevitable that people will agree to limit their
freedom and create a powerful state to rule.[2] He believes people are
rational, which is to say they understand that even though they have

infinite freedom *in theory* in the state of nature, they will actually end up impinging on one another's freedom. You can steal my food, but someone else will steal it from you. By limiting our own freedom, Hobbes thinks, we have a practical enjoyment of more. You may not be able to take my apple, but if you get an apple yourself, then we can both enjoy our apples in comfort. In other words, citizens create the state in order to provide for their interests and the state's right to govern citizens is based on the rational consent of the inhabitants, rather than some inborn right of the governors to govern.

Hobbes makes a "bottom-up" argument. The state arises from the will of the people. The other side of this debate, the "top-down" argument, argues that social orders are given and do not depend on the will of the people. Cicero,* a Roman politician and jurist, is perhaps the best-known thinker in this top-down tradition. Justice, argues Cicero, "is not a product of human thought, nor is it an enactment of peoples, but something eternal which rules the entire universe."[3]

Academic Influences

Burke was deeply influenced by the French thinker Charles-Louis de Secondat, Baron de La Brède et de Montesquieu* (known simply as Montesquieu). Not only did Burke and Montesquieu agree on the general purpose of government, they also agreed on the ways change should be carried out in government. Montesquieu argued, "When a prince wants to make great changes in his nation, he must reform by laws what is established by laws and change by manners what is established by manners."[4] This means that when a ruler wants to make a political change, the ruler must tailor this change to the nature of the society they are changing. There is no universal law that can sweep over every nation. Burke called Montesquieu "the greatest genius, which has enlightened this age."[5]

Burke was also influenced by the literary techniques of the rationalist* thinkers he was arguing against. For example, he twisted the concept of the state of nature to argue against it. Unlike Hobbes, Burke did not see the state of nature as a pre-social situation. He thought of it as the actual state. He argued that man did not will the state, "but God willed ... the state." And so every aspect of the state that may initially seem irrational is both established by God and entirely natural.[6]

Burke argued that God and history gave humanity its governmental institutions. The king does not rule because the ruled have consented to it; the king rules because God ordered society this way. To Burke, the fact that a system of government exists makes it self-evidently the best system. The act of rational inquiry into the basis of the state, which was made popular in the Enlightenment, was unproductive at best and threatening to the natural order at worst. Thinkers like Burke and Montesquieu saw states, even with their seeming imperfections, as the natural products of different societies. This is a pragmatic* view, as there is a French state that works for the French, an English state that works for the English, and an American state that works for the Americans. In other words, there is no such thing as a universal ideal.

NOTES

1   Norman Hampson, *The Enlightenment: An Evaluation of its Assumptions, Attitudes and Values* (London: Penguin, 1990).

2   Thomas Hobbes, *Leviathan*, ed. with an Introduction and Notes J. C. A. Gaskin (Oxford: Oxford University Press, 1998), 142.

3   Cicero, quoted in Christopher J. Insole, "Burke and the Natural Law," in *The Cambridge Companion to Edmund Burke*, eds. David Dwan and Christopher J. Insole (Cambridge: Cambridge University Press, 2012), 121.

4   Montesquieu, *The Spirit of the Laws*, eds. Anne M. Cohler, Basia C. Miller, and Harold S. Stone (Cambridge: Cambridge University Press, 1989), 315.

5   Edmund Burke, "An Essay Towards an Abridgement of the English History," in *The Works of the Right Honourable Edmund Burke in Twelve Volumes*, Volume the Seventh (London: John C. Nimmo, 1887), 316.

6   Edmund Burke, *Reflections on the Revolution in France*, ed. with an Introduction and Notes by L. G. Mitchell, Oxford World's Classics (Oxford: Oxford University Press, 1993 and 2009), 98.

MODULE 3
THE PROBLEM

KEY POINTS

- Burke asked: Is the French Revolution* a good thing, and ought its principles be reproduced in other European states?
- Radicals argued that societies should be organized into perfect systems to preserve man's "natural rights."*
- Burke said the radical idea that society can be made into a paradise was both dangerous and false.

Core Question

Edmund Burke's *Reflections on the Revolution in France* was written to answer two core questions: Was the French Revolution a good thing for France? And would it be a good thing for Britain? The theoretical line of inquiry underlying both questions is: Is it possible or desirable to tear down a government and rebuild it along brand new lines? The book was in no way a debate. Burke approached these questions with his answers already in mind. He felt that the French Revolution was an atrocity and that the traditional form of government in France and its institutions should be defended. To him the Revolution's radical, liberal Enlightenment-inspired* ideas of popular sovereignty* should be kept out of Britain at all costs.

In a letter he wrote in 1791, entitled "Thoughts on French Affairs," Burke brings to light the importance of assessing French revolutionary principles. He notes that "the present revolution in France … is a Revolution of doctrine and theoretic dogma," with an almost-religious "spirit of proselytism."*[1] In other words, Burke thought the ideals of the Revolution were likely to spread throughout Europe if

> **❝** I see the ardour for liberty catching and spreading, a general amendment beginning in human affairs, the dominion of kings changed for the dominion of laws, and the dominion of priests giving way to the dominion of reason and conscience. **❞**
>
> Richard Price, *A Discourse on the Love of Our Country*

they were not discredited. Burke referred to the French Revolution and its underlying Enlightenment ideas as a "plague," which required "the most severe quarantine."*[2]

The Participants

The Revolution caused enormous debate in Britain. Burke saw himself as writing in direct response to those who were excited about the possibility of similar radical political reform, especially the Welsh preacher and philosopher Dr. Richard Price.* Price preached a sermon, which he called *A Discourse on the Love of Our Country*, which praised the French Revolution. In it Price wrote, "I have lived to see thirty millions of people, indignant and resolute, spurning at slavery, and demanding liberty, who have deposed their king and established a government for themselves."[3] In other words, Price sees the French Revolution as historically just and righteous. The Revolution Society,* a group of London radicals that Price belonged to, voted to send a message to the French National Assembly,* "rejoicing in every triumph of liberty and justice over arbitrary power, [offering] … their congratulations on the Revolution."[4]

The most important thing about Price's sermon, however, is not the congratulations he sent to France. It was rather his implication that France had joined in a revolutionary tradition started by England 100 years before when the Glorious Revolution of 1688* deposed King James II* and replaced him with William III.* Price wrote, "After sharing in the benefits of one revolution, I have been … witness to two other Revolutions, both glorious."[5] Price argued that the Glorious Revolution had made the king of England the servant of the people, so the English people in effect had supreme authority over their own land. Price argued that the Glorious Revolution gave the English three key rights: "1. To choose our own governors. 2. To cashier them for misconduct. 3. To frame a government for ourselves."[6] To cashier meant to remove people from power. Effectively, these three "rights" gave the English citizen authority and power over his government.

All three of the rights mentioned by Price were inspired by the ideas of the Enlightenment. Enlightenment thinkers wanted to prove that governments exist to serve the people, not the other way around. For example, the English liberal philosopher John Locke* wrote, "the liberty of man, in society, is to be under no other legislative power, but that established, by consent, in the commonwealth."[7] Consent is the critical concept here. The moment the governed man withdraws his consent, then the government becomes illegitimate. The entire basis of government is not found in nature, God, or tradition. There is no way for a government to rule legitimately without the consent of the governed.

Locke's views were part of a major trend. There were many thinkers who believed that government was the product of a contract made by the people. Therefore the people had a right to control and dissolve their government. These ideas were extremely liberal by the standards of seventeenth- and eighteenth-century Europe, where concepts such as the "divine right of kings"* (that authority for a king to rule had been given directly by God) still held some sway. The intellectual environment of Burke's time was becoming increasingly unhappy with concepts such as divine right as a justification for authority. Enlightenment thinkers such as Locke and Price would only accept a society where the government was no more than the agent of the people's will. Burke rejected this view wholesale. He wrote that the only contract in society was the contract between man and God to keep society intact. In this sense, *Reflections* ran against the intellectual fashion of the day.

The Contemporary Debate

Burke's rejection of the French Revolution and its Enlightenment ideals was not completely straightforward. It had political and intellectual dimensions. His own party, the Whigs,* was split on its view of the Revolution. Leading Whig Charles James Fox* agreed with Price's sermon. Fox said of the Revolution, "How much the greatest event it is that ever happened in the world!"[8] Burke knew the Revolution had supporters in many areas of British society. It had the support of the elite like Fox and the general public like Price. Burke saw himself as leading a counter-attack in favor of tradition and government that already existed. Burke's assault on Enlightenment principles was designed to make them look dangerous. His intellectual mission was political.

Burke was part of an intellectual school called the "Counter-Enlightenment."* The term was used by the twentieth-century Russian-British philosopher Isaiah Berlin* to bring together all the thinkers who were against the Enlightenment. However, Burke did not see himself as a member of any particular school of thought. His only mission was to defend the English constitution.* The thing that distinguishes Burke from his fellow reactionaries* against the Enlightenment was that he wasn't just arguing for authority. He was a constitutional thinker, trying to work out what government is and should be.

In his analysis of the Counter-Enlightenment, Berlin notes that Burke was "not theocratic, nor absolutist, not addicted to extremes," like other thinkers in the Counter-Enlightenment, such as French nobleman and philosopher Joseph de Maistre.* Berlin continues,

"Burke's denunciation of abstract ideas … and … his total opposition to the liberation of human beings from the artificial and removable shell of tradition, social texture … make him a member of the counter-enlightenment."[9] Burke, in other words, was a political pragmatist, meaning he favored what worked in the real world, rather than what appeared to work in theory.

NOTES

1   Edmund Burke, "Thoughts on French Affairs," in *The Works of the Right Honourable Edmund Burke in Twelve Volumes, Volume the Fourth* (London: John C. Nimmo, 1887), 313–78.

2   Edmund Burke, *Reflections on the Revolution in France*, ed. with an Introduction and Notes by L. G. Mitchell, Oxford World's Classics (Oxford: Oxford University Press, 1993 and 2009), 89.

3   Richard Price, *A Discourse on the Love of Our Country* (London: T. Cadell, 1789), accessed January 15, 2015. http://lf-oll.s3.amazonaws.com/titles/368/1290_Bk.pdf, 49.

4   Price, "Appendix" to *Discourse*, 13.

5   Price, *Discourse*, 49.

6   Burke, *Reflections*, 16.

7   John Locke, "Of Civil Government. Book II: The Second Treatise," *Two Treatises of Government and a Letter Concerning Toleration* (New Haven, CT: Yale University Press, 2003), 110.

8   James R. Arnold, *The Aftermath of the French Revolution* (Minneapolis, MN: Twenty-First Century Books, 2009), 95.

9   Isaiah Berlin, "Joseph de Maistre and the Origins of Fascism," in *The Crooked Timber of Humanity; Chapters in the History of Ideas*, ed. Henry Hardy (Princeton, NJ: Princeton University Press, 2013), 131–2.

MODULE 4
THE AUTHOR'S CONTRIBUTION

KEY POINTS

- Burke argued that the radical reforms associated with the French Revolution* should be kept out of Britain at any cost.

- *Reflections* is a key work of the Counter-Enlightenment* and provides a thorough rejection of government based on completely theoretical ideas.

- Burke's criticism of the idea of creating perfect government parodies the "Enlightenment"* philosophy.

Author's Aims

Edmund Burke's aims in *Reflections on the Revolution in France* were political rather than philosophical. His idea was to show that the intellectually fashionable notions of liberty and popular sovereignty* would bring disaster to Britain should they ever take root there. Burke's intention was to defend British politics by discrediting the French Revolution as immoral and impractical. His more theoretical intention was to reject abstract political reasoning—which he called "metaphysic"*—as a valid method for political investigation. Burke put forward an anti-rationalist* "counter-theory" of politics against Enlightenment reasoning. Burke's theory was that the existing social order was ordained by God and was natural. This natural society had come about as the result of many generations of partnership between men and God. He wrote, "This law is not subject to the will of those, who by an obligation above them, and infinitely superior, are bound to submit their will to that law."[1]

> ❝ I should therefore suspend my congratulations on the new liberty of France, until I was informed how it had been combined with government; with public force; with the discipline and obedience of armies; with the collection of an effective and well-distributed revenue; with morality and religion; with the solidity of property; with peace and order; with civil and social manners. ❞
>
> Edmund Burke, *Reflections on the Revolution in France*

To Burke the philosophy underpinning the French Revolution was dangerous because it was so seductive. It told the common man he deserved to rule as much as the king did and that traditional power structures were not logical. Burke was not interested in how traditional power structures came to be—he was only interested in what worked. So the belief that God had decided man should obey the king did not have to be based on sound principles. It was only important that society stayed functional and orderly. Any threat to these principles, no matter how well intentioned, was a threat to functional society.

Approach

Because Burke wrote *Reflections* to convince readers, rather than to make a logical philosophical argument, his work is more persuasive that it is rational. That is to say, Burke deliberately wrote the book to shock and convince rather than to argue every point of a position, looking to make sure it could stand up to future inspection. Burke was driven to write *Reflections* when the French aristocrat Charles-Jean-François Depont* asked him what he thought of the Revolution. So the book was written in the style of a letter to a friend, meaning Burke could speak to his audience on a more direct and personal level. Burke calls this "the freedom of epistolary intercourse," which refers to the act of two friends exchanging letters. He describes how he wrote *Reflections* by "[throwing] out my thoughts and [expressing] my feelings just as they arise in my mind, with very little attention to formal method."[2]

Abandoning the form of the essay, which is a balanced academic inquiry into a topic to uncover its true nature, Burke was able to take a less balanced view. The "epistolary" style meant he could pick his own points of emphasis, ignore counter-arguments and use poetic devices such as imagery* and metaphor.* He wanted to leave the reader with a fear of revolutionary ideas and an overall feeling of disgust at the French Revolution. For example, when discussing the arrest of the French Queen, Marie Antoinette,* Burke focuses on the image of an innocent woman stolen from her bedroom by a bloodstained "band of cruel ruffians."[3]

Burke chose to ignore the legitimate grievances of those "ruffians" against the monarchy,* preferring to caricature them to create emotional sympathy for the French ruling classes. Descriptive passages such as this show that *Reflections* is not meant to be a structured dismantling of revolutionary ideas, nor is it a piece of philosophy. Instead, it is a piece of rhetoric*—a persuasive argument—designed to counter the equally rhetorical ideas about man's natural rights put forward by Enlightenment political thinkers.

Contribution in Context

Burke's argument had a lot in common with a number of other figures of the "Counter-Enlightenment," especially French philosopher Joseph de Maistre.* In an essay on the Revolution de Maistre asks, "The people is sovereign, they say; and over whom? Over itself apparently. The people is therefore subject. There is surely something equivocal here, if not an error, for the people that *commands* is not the people that *obeys*."[4] De Maistre is pointing out, much as Burke does, that a rationally perfect government where the people rules over itself will just create a whole new set of problems. For example, if the people want to redistribute all property to solve the problem of inequality, it can be seen that this could produce new problems about people's motivations to work. But in Burke and de Maistre's view, the institutions that already exist can deal with inequality. They may not do it perfectly, but they do so without causing new problems.

In *Reflections* Burke shows both the development of his thoughts on the French Revolution and on the nature of politics in general. His pragmatic* stance against rationalism* runs through his entire body of work. His argument in favor of traditionalism and pragmatism can be traced back to one of his first works, *A Vindication of Natural Society*, in 1756. In the preface to *Vindication*—which was a satire of Enlightenment-style rationalism—Burke said, "nothing could be more fatal to Mankind than [the] Success of philosophers in attacking the traditional institutions that underpin political society."[5] His immediate reaction to the French Revolution, recorded in a letter to a friend sent in 1789, suggests his skepticism. He wrote that the French "must have a Strong hand like that of their former masters to coerce them," otherwise they would be "not fit for Liberty."[6] Burke's skepticism grew as the Revolution went on and he condemned it completely as it turned into The Terror of 1792 to 1794.

NOTES

1   Edmund Burke, *Reflections on the Revolution in France*, ed. with an Introduction and Notes by L. G. Mitchell, Oxford World's Classics (Oxford: Oxford University Press, 1993 and 2009), 97.

2   Burke, *Reflections*, 10.

3   Burke, *Reflections*, 71.

4   Joseph de Maistre, "Against Rousseau," *The Collected Works of Joseph de Maistre*, ed. Richard Lebrun (Charlottesville, VA: Intelex, 2008), 44.

5   Edmund Burke, *A Vindication of Natural Society: Or, A View of the Miseries and Evils Arising to Mankind from Every Species of Artificial Society,* ed. Frank N. Pagano (Indianapolis, IN: Liberty Fund, 1982, first published 1756), 2.

6   Edmund Burke, quoted in F. P. Lock, *Edmund Burke: Volume II: 1784–1797* (Oxford: Oxford University Press, 2009), 244.

SECTION 2
IDEAS

MAIN IDEAS

KEY POINTS

- Burke's main theme is the need for tradition, inheritance, and prejudice. He saw these as the three essential ingredients of a strong society.

- *Reflections* argues that European societies should cherish their inherited institutions and only reform them slowly and after long historical experience.

- In *Reflections* Burke uses emotional language to convince his reader. It is more an opinionated work intended to change people's minds than it is a work of philosophy.

Key Themes

Edmund Burke's key themes in *Reflections on the Revolution in France* are: the importance of "prejudice," "presumption," and "prescription" to good government; and the threat to this posed by radical ideas. By "prejudice," Burke means the way people automatically think their existing institutions are legitimate and correct. So, France, for example, would be "prejudiced" to support Catholicism* for the sole reason that it has a history of Catholicism. "Presumption" means the idea that things are as they always have been. So we are in favor of existing institutions because they have always worked. "Prescription" means that institutions are to be obeyed because they demand obedience and it provides the basis of the authority of all these inherited institutions. This leads to the idea that society is inherited, not invented. Each generation takes responsibility for the institutions it inherits from previous generations and preserves them for future generations.

> **❝** To avoid the evils of inconstancy and versatility, ten thousand times worse than those of obstinacy and the blindest prejudice, we have consecrated the state, that no man should approach to look into its defects or corruptions but with due caution; that he should never dream of beginning its reformation by its subversion. **❞**
>
> Edmund Burke, *Reflections on the Revolution in France*

Pure rationalism* and science are about exposing assumptions and questioning authority. So Enlightenment* ideas of rationalism and scientific explanations of society destroy Burke's conservative* ideas of good government based on prescription, presumption, and prejudice. Burke believed that, because they were not rooted in existing institutions, "the pretended rights of [political] theorists" could never be practically applied, since "in proportion as they are metaphysically true, they are morally and politically false."[1] By this Burke means that government is not a science with exact answers. For example, he can understand why people may question why the Church is an integral part of society. To him, the fact that it *is* an integral part of society makes it too important to be experimented with. For Burke, political theory based on pure reason and with pretensions to science was unable to answer the questions posed by real-life politics. Why? For the very reason that it had no grounding in real-life politics.

Burke also shows the danger posed to his concept of good society by radical reform. He has both a specific argument against allowing French Revolution* principles into England and a more general philosophical argument against *all* radical, revolutionary political change. To Burke, revolutionary change is an enormous threat to property and society.

Exploring the Ideas

Burke's key themes—the three forces that establish good government, and the one force that destroys it—provide a workable theory of politics based on a total disregard for the idea of "theory." Abstract ideas of what may work perfectly are ditched in favor of the idea of "history"—real evidence of what works well enough. For Burke, France as envisioned by its revolutionaries stood for a state that had discarded its history and tradition in favor of a radical, theory-driven government.

Burke's most enduring idea is that, though universal rights* sounds like a great idea and may make sense rationally, they simply will not work. He wrote that universal rights will be "refracted from their straight line" if they are applied to the structure of political society and that this will produce unintended negative consequences.[2] What Burke means by this is that while ideas such as "government by consent"* may seem attractive, they will become distorted in practice. For example, a society based on taking orders from a king may be far from perfect, and some kings are better than others, but what if a thinker decides a better society will be one that is completely equal and where everyone can vote on everything. Then, all of a sudden, everyone is too busy voting on things to grow their food or go to work and society grinds to a halt. So the king's rule may not have been ideal, but at least society functioned. This is what Burke means when he says that rigorous application of an abstract right to "equality" may cause a breakdown in authority and a worse life for all.

Once you have understood Burke's criticism of the Enlightenment's "scientific" approach to politics—where politics is investigated as a kind of universal truth to be experimented upon and perfected—it is easy to see why he was so upset by the victory of the revolutionaries. He writes, "the age of chivalry* is gone," meaning the stable state and refined manners of the old regime have disappeared. They have been replaced, continues Burke, by the manners, "of sophisters, economists, and calculators … and the glory of Europe is extinguished forever."[3] In other words, the stability of a real, working state has been sacrificed for "pure reason," which may be attractive, but will not work. Burke asked, "what is the use of discussing a man's abstract right to anything, if he does not already have it?"[4]

Burke does not value the age of chivalry and its institutions simply because they are old. He values traditional French political institutions because they are the product of generations of experience governing France. He wrote, "Old establishments are tried by their effects … they are not often constructed after any theory: theories are rather drawn from them."[5] By this he means that existing institutions in society—from forms of government to religion—may not be perfect, but they have worked for long enough to keep society going. If they are to be changed, then they ought to be changed slowly.

Burke preferred to think of rights as an "entailed* inheritance" of religion, law, and institutions.[6] When the French attempted to create a new set of laws by pure reason they abandoned their divinely sanctioned natural law* that had been given to them by God and history. This natural law, and the institutions that it sanctioned, adequately if imperfectly provided for the necessities of daily life. For this reason, Burke argues, France "has abandoned her interest, that she might prostitute her virtue."[7] For Burke, the answers to political questions such as what are our rights, and what is the basis of a well-ordered society, are universally found in history. They can be found by examining how generations upon generations have answered these questions, rather than looking to theory. Burke saw that as dreaming answers up from nothing.

Language and Expression

Burke was writing a piece of propaganda, so he wrote to conjure up an emotion as much as to express an idea. The British-American political activist Thomas Paine,* a contemporary critic of Burke, commented on *Reflections*: "I cannot consider Mr. Burke's book in scarcely any other light than a dramatic performance," going on to suggest Burke also considered his work a piece of drama, "by the [poetic] liberties he has taken of omitting some facts, distorting others, and making the whole machinery bend to produce a stage effect."[8] The nub of Paine's criticism of Burke is that Burke had come up with his answer before he started writing and that he was more concerned with convincing people than presenting any kind of neutral overview. For example, Burke uses disgusted language to talk about the French National Assembly,* calling it a "profane burlesque, and [an] abominable perversion."[9] He does not have evidence the Assembly is a burlesque (a grotesque parody), but uses this charged language to give his reader a sense of terror and revulsion. This tone— light on evidence and full of emphatic, emotional language—can be confusing for modern readers, who can find themselves unable to get past Burke's apparent rage. The American intellectual historian Frank M. Turner* writes, "To champion prudence over perfection is in and of itself a hard sell, and Burke did not make this task any easier for himself" by his over-the-top writing style.[10] Turner continues that the style can make readers think of Burke as a shrill reactionary and so can find themselves taking against him.

NOTES

1 Edmund Burke, *Reflections on the Revolution in France*, ed. with an Introduction and Notes by L. G. Mitchell, Oxford World's Classics (Oxford: Oxford University Press, 1993 and 2009), 62.

2 Burke, *Reflections*, 61.

3 Burke, *Reflections*, 76.

4 Burke, *Reflections*, 61.

5 Burke, *Reflections*, 173.

6 Burke, *Reflections*, 29.

7   Burke, *Reflections*, 37.

8   Thomas Paine, *Rights of Man: Being an Answer to Mr. Burke's Attack on the French Revolution* (London: J. S. Jordan, 1791), 39.

9   Burke, *Reflections*, 53.

10 Frank M. Turner, "Edmund Burke: The Political Actor Thinking," Introduction to Edmund Burke, *Reflections on the Revolution in France*, ed. Frank M. Turner (New Haven, CT: Yale University Press, 2003), xiv.

MODULE 6
SECONDARY IDEAS

KEY POINTS

- Burke presents a historical view of England's revolution, known as the Glorious Revolution,* to support his theoretical argument. He argues that the Glorious Revolution made England safe from radical change.

- Burke disagrees with the idea that the Glorious Revolution showed England was ready for the rule of the people. He argues that it actually demonstrated how England values its traditions above revolutionary ideas.

- Burke presents a conservative* theory of economics that can be seen as an early argument against the government interfering in the economy. This paved the way for later economics thinkers such as Milton Friedman* and Friedrich von Hayek.*

Other Ideas

One of the most important sub-themes in *Reflections on the Revolution in France* is Edmund Burke's take on England's "Glorious Revolution." This revolution of 1688 had been used by political thinkers such as Dr. Richard Price* to show that revolutionary ideas had already been established in England. Price believed that the Glorious Revolution had a lot in common with the French Revolution.* He wrote that he was overjoyed to have lived to see the French people "indignant and resolute, spurning slavery, and demanding liberty with an irresistible voice, setting themselves free of an arbitrary monarch." According to Price, this was very similar to the way the English had acted during the Glorious Revolution when they rose up to overthrow the Roman Catholic* King James II* and replace him with the Protestant* William III.*

> 66 The pretended rights of these theorists are all
> extremes: and in proportion as they are metaphysically
> true, they are morally and politically false. The rights of
> men are in a sort of *middle*, incapable of definition, but
> not impossible to be discerned. 99
>
> Edmund Burke, *Reflections on the Revolution in France*

In the aftermath of the Revolution of 1688 the English Parliament* passed the Bill of Rights, based on the Declaration of Right,* which stipulated, among other things, that: no Roman Catholics shall rule England, and the king may not suspend laws.[1] To Price, this represented a limitation of the king's power *by* the people, turning the king into a servant *of* the people. Burke however, was of the opposite view and thought that the Glorious Revolution rather showed that England valued its traditions (namely its heritage of Protestantism since Henry VIII) above radical ideas of turning the country back towards the Roman Catholic faith being introduced by a Roman Catholic monarch.

Exploring the Ideas
Burke argues that the Glorious Revolution *protected* England from radical change, while the French Revolution *subjected* France to radical change. For Burke, the Glorious Revolution was not an act of destruction and rebuilding. He maintained that the revolutionaries "[secured] the religion, laws, and liberties that had been long possessed, and had only been lately endangered."[2] Burke believes that the history of English liberty—from the "Magna Charta* to the Declaration of Right"—did not involve abstract "rights of man," but has been a straight-line of "inheritance derived to us from our forefathers."[3]

Even though there was a democratic "moment" in English history in 1688, when Parliament dethroned the unpopular reigning monarch in favor of another, Burke argues this moment protected the course of English history from possible ruin. Burke held that, "Instead of a right to choose our own governors," the Revolution established the right for the English to enjoy a stable monarchy and the "peace, quiet, and security" that accompany it.[4] The Glorious Revolution changed the power of the monarchy. It also emphasized the ongoing importance of the monarchy. It did not declare a new government based on an ill-defined principle of popular sovereignty.

Burke felt it absurd that English radicals saw a connection between the Glorious Revolution and the French Revolution. To Burke, the Revolution of 1688 was a special case where drastic action was taken to ensure regularity in future. His view of the Glorious Revolution shows that Burke is not a simple-minded reactionary who unthinkingly supports whatever is traditional. He has a theory of legitimate political change, based on slow, gradual alteration of constitutions that have already led to long-term stability. The Declaration of Right did establish some limitation on the power of the king, but it could not be taken out of context and used to establish some general principle that the king is, in fact, the servant of the population. In Burke's eyes, politics is much more complicated than that.

Overlooked

Reflections is not just a work of political thought, because Burke also writes as an economist. He saw potential for the French Revolution to destroy the French economy. He examines the consequences of the decision by the National Assembly,* as the post-revolutionary government was called, to confiscate and redistribute Church property among the people. Burke thought this was immoral because it disrupted the "natural" distribution of property. He also thought it was doomed to produce inflation.*

Burke's aversion to government intervention in the economy was rooted in his belief that "the laws of commerce are inexorable, and that the likely victims of any attempted interference are the very people who are the objects of reformers' compassion."[5] He believed the economics of supply and demand,* which were similar to the theories of the Scottish political philosopher Adam Smith,* were natural and good. In Burke's view, the French revolutionary government interfered in the natural functioning of markets and upset the moral and economic balance of their society. This allows us to see the complexity of Burke's reasoning and reminds us he was a subtle operator, able to apply both economic and historical thinking.

NOTES

1   Heather Campbell, *The Britannica Guide to Political and Social Movements that Changed the Modern World* (New York: Britannica Educational Publishing, 2010), 40.

2   Edmund Burke, *Reflections on the Revolution in France*, ed. with an Introduction and Notes by L. G. Mitchell, Oxford World's Classics (Oxford: Oxford University Press, 1993 and 2009), 32.

3   Burke, *Reflections*, 29.

4   Burke, *Reflections*, 15.

5   Norman P. Barry, "The Political Economy of Edmund Burke," in *Edmund Burke: His Life and Legacy*, ed. Ian Crowe (Dublin: Four Courts Press, 1997), 109.

ACHIEVEMENT

KEY POINTS

- Burke provided a conservative* argument against radical* ideologies, and remains a key source of conservative thought today.

- *Reflections* addressed a "hot" political issue and made an immediate impact because it was widely read by English politicians and the general public.

- The achievement of *Reflections* has been limited throughout its history because it appears to be a totally anti-liberal* work. This perception has led to strong criticism and ongoing misunderstanding of Burke.

Assessing the Argument

Edmund Burke's *Reflections on the Revolution in France* sold 17,500 copies in its first year and caused a great deal of discussion and controversy.[1] This commercial success also meant the book's ideas had a lasting impact. Over time, *Reflections* began to be seen as "a warning of the perils of rootless rationalism"* and a serious reminder that institutions are often too complex for individuals to grasp completely.[2]

Burke's significance to contemporary debate also goes beyond his counter-revolutionary theory. The twentieth-century American political scientist Samuel P. Huntington* wrote that "all the analysts of conservatism … unite in identifying Edmund Burke as the conservative archetype."*[3] While Burke may have originally written *Reflections* to—as British historian Frank O'Gorman* writes—"argue the [French] Revolution out of existence,"[4] it has nonetheless gained a timeless quality. Specifically, according to Huntington, conservatives

> ❝ Burke, more than any other writer of the day, succeeded in defining for his own and later generations the new political order arising in France and the danger it posed to existing British and European social and political institutions and values ... When Burke died in 1797, no other writer of the era of the French Revolution had produced a work of more lasting transatlantic influence. ❞
>
> Frank M. Turner, "The Political Actor Thinking," Introduction to *Reflections*

note Burke's pragmatic* approach to politics as an organic process. His lasting criticism was not of democracy,* but of the unexpected consequences of radical political change based on pure theory.

This meant Burke remained popular throughout the nineteenth century in Britain and America and enjoyed "an exalted reputation in literature, history, and politics."[5] Since then, Burke's importance has grown even more. The contemporary political commentator Peter J. Stanlis* suggests, "Burke's reply to the totalitarian* doctrines of the French Revolution has a special significance to twentieth century man."[6]

Achievement in Context

When *Reflections* was first published it was extremely popular and ignited a debate between Burke and English radicals. Burke was widely mocked, in particular in the two years after its publication in 1790. He was ridiculed by supporters of the French Revolution, when popular euphoria in Britain about French political developments was still visible. Burke's biographer, the Canadian academic F. P. Lock,* describes a political cartoon of Burke "kneeling adoringly" in front of Marie Antoinette, the deposed Queen of

France, "who treads on a cloud." Even during his own time Burke was seen as a sycophant—someone who flatters influential or wealthy people to win favor from them.[7]

In 1792, the noble goals of the French Revolution somehow got lost and were turned into paranoid terror. Civil liberties were suspended and more than 40,000 lives were lost in the repression of those said to be enemies of the state. This period, known as The Terror,* turned Burke into something of a prophet. Burke's fellow parliamentarian Lord Dundas* wrote: "It was reserved for the illuminated and comprehensive mind of Mr. Burke alone, to foresee what must be its fatal and necessary consequences ... time ... has stamped his predictions, and verified them by events."[8]

Limitations

Surprisingly for an opinionated work that was unashamedly rooted in the events of its time, *Reflections* has transcended the 1790s and acquired a more timeless status. It has often been applied to the study and practice of politics. But, *Reflections*'s popularity has been limited because it has been seen as overly shrill and anti-liberal. This is why some modern readers, especially those who take liberal democracy for granted, find Burke hard to read. They see him as a hysterical anti-democratic rather than a skeptic who rejected the radical notions of the French Revolution. Burke historian Frank M. Turner* tells an anecdote about one of his students who remarked: "This book is offensive, really offensive!"[9] Burke appears to fundamentally disagree with a number of key liberal democratic assumptions. For example, he dismisses democracy, suggesting, "The will of the many, and their interest, must very often differ" and that "the constitution of a kingdom [is not] a problem of arithmetic."[10] Burke's politics are not necessarily anti-democratic; they are fundamentally pragmatic. This pragmatism led him to be skeptical of *any* program of reform. Burke's immediate political conclusions are, by definition, of their time and place, but his pragmatism is something that has relevance across time.

NOTES

1   F. P. Lock, *Edmund Burke: Volume II: 1784–1797* (Oxford: Oxford University Press, 2009), 332.

2   Robert Rhodes James, "The Relevance of Edmund Burke," in *Edmund Burke: His Life and Legacy*, ed. Ian Crowe (Dublin: Four Courts Press, 1997), 149.

3   Samuel P. Huntington, "Conservatism as Ideology," *American Political Science Review* 51, no. 2 (1957): 456.

4   Frank O'Gorman, *Edmund Burke: His Political Philosophy* (London: George Allen & Unwin, 1973), 141.

5   Peter J. Stanlis, "Edmund Burke in the Twentieth Century," in *The Relevance of Edmund Burke*, ed. Peter J. Stanlis (New York: P. J. Kennedy, 1964), 29.

6   Stanlis, "Burke in the Twentieth Century," 45.

7   Lock, *Edmund Burke,* 334.

8   Great Britain, *The Parliamentary Register or History of the Proceedings and Debates of the House of Commons* (London: J. Debrett, 1794), 180.

9   Frank M. Turner, "Edmund Burke: The Political Actor Thinking," Introduction to Edmund Burke, *Reflections on the Revolution in France*, ed. Frank M. Turner (New Haven, CT: Yale University Press, 2003), xiii.

10   Burke, *Reflections*, 52.

PLACE IN THE AUTHOR'S WORK

KEY POINTS

- Burke wrote about all of the big issues of his day, including the monarchy,* imperialism,* democratization,* government corruption, and revolution.

- Burke supported the American Revolution,* but opposed the French Revolution.* His emphasis was on pragmatism* in both cases.

- *Reflections* is Burke's most famous work and is still widely read by political theorists and politicians.

Positioning

Edmund Burke wrote *Reflections on the Revolution in France* late in his life when he was already in his sixties. It was one of the last works of a very productive career. His other writing touched on many subjects, from the contexts of revolution to imperialism and democracy. However, a lot of Burke's most important writing was not even published. It took the form of speeches given to the House of Commons, the lower house in the British Parliament.* British historian Frank O'Gorman* writes that Burke was "not a philosopher at all [but] a practical politician and a propagandist."[1] In other words, Burke did not write for the sake of writing or thinking. He wrote with a particular political outcome in mind.

Burke's pragmatic anti-rationalism* is woven through all his work. His central theme of traditionalism and pragmatism can be traced back to his first book, *A Vindication of Natural Society*, published in 1756. This book appears to be an Enlightenment* textbook, but Burke makes it clear in the preface that it is actually a parody. In

> **❝** If there be one fact in the world perfectly clear, it is this: 'that the disposition of the people of America is wholly averse to any other than a free government' ... If any ask me what a free government is, I answer, that, for any practical purpose, it is what the people think so—and that they, and not I, are the natural, lawful, and competent judges of this matter. **❞**
>
> Edmund Burke, "Letter to John Farr and John Harris, Esqrs, Sheriffs of the City of Bristol, on the Affairs of America, April 3, 1777"

Vindication Burke satirizes writers who "pretend to exalt the mind of man, by proving him no better than a beast," and who claim to "increase our piety, and our reliance on God, by exploding his providence, and insisting he is neither just nor good?"[2] In other words, Burke mocks those who use abstract reason to make a case for political authority. This kind of thinking is absurd, to Burke, because in his view man is lifted up by living in society and taking part in tradition. All of Burke's work is informed by his belief that the purpose of politics is not to satisfy the interests of individuals, but to preserve a social order that, coming out of the past, addresses the needs of present and future generations.

Integration

It may feel contradictory that Burke wrote in support of the American Revolution, yet against the French. In fact he uses the same principles for both arguments. In his 1777 "Letter to John Farr and John Harris, Esqrs" Burke was supportive of American liberty. He believed that "the disposition of the people of America is wholly averse to any other than a free government."[3] Burke felt Britain should not treat America like a colony, because they would not put up with being treated that way. For Burke, this particular piece of pragmatism was right for

America, because he believed it suited American society. The liberty loved by Americans, however, was not "abstract liberty, like other mere abstractions," but real-life liberty specifically focusing on issues of taxation and property rights.[4]

Burke recognized that it was lawful for Britain to tax America, but argued that it "is not reconcilable to any ideas of liberty, much less with theirs and … has kindled this flame that is ready to consume us."[5] In other words, the Americans' idea of liberty is not tied to an abstract idea, but to whether or not they own their property. Burke saw *this* desire for liberty as natural. He hated and feared the same drive for liberty in Europe because he believed that it did not suit Europeans, who already possessed a body of rights, inherited from history. Burke modified his thinking depending on the political issue at hand but, once he had decided a political position on an issue, he stuck to it doggedly.

Burke's writings about the British Empire* follow the same theme as his revolutionary writings. Burke was chair of the parliamentary select committee investigating British misrule in East India. When the former Governor-General of Bengal and director of the East India Company, Warren Hastings*, was on trial for gross misrule of India (in a case that dragged on from 1788 to 1795), Burke was lead prosecutor. His attack was passionate and once again consistent with his principles. Burke made a famous speech and said: "If we undertake to govern the inhabitants of such a country we must govern them upon their own principles and maxims, and not upon ours."[6] To Burke, ruling abroad does not mean imposing the will of the central state, but the taking on of an enormous responsibility. Burke highlights "the care [with which] we ought to handle people so delicate."[7]

An examination of all the topics to which Burke applied his mind shows that he is not a tyrant, nor a reactionary. He is a political skeptic, who always urges caution to those who would like to change the systems that are in place and which he believes generally work.

Significance

The American historian Frank M. Turner credits the enduring impact of *Reflections* to the way it can be used as a framework to look at all political issues. Turner said: "Burke's argument achieved lasting authority because even though he directed it against the revolution in France, he shaped it as a more general criticism of arbitrary political power informed by a zeal for ideas."[8] Burke's 1796 "Second Letter on a Regicide Peace" criticized the all-powerful post-revolutionary French state where all appearance of liberty had disappeared—at least to Burke. Talking of how the French revolutionary government seemed to be all-powerful, Burke said, "The state is all in all, the state has dominion and conquest for its sole objects—dominion over minds by proselytism, over bodies by arms."[9] As Turner put it the "zeal for ideas" of abstract liberty had led to a state of affairs where there was actually no liberty.

Burke rose from relatively humble beginnings to succeed as a politician who influenced a number of important political debates in Britain, such as limiting the power of the monarchy and dealing with corruption among the governing classes in India. Burke's writing has had a lasting influence because it tapped into a fundamental truth about politics. Politics is the realm of experience, history, and care, and to treat it as subservient to passing intellectual fashion is to risk its destruction. This is why Burke is remembered today as one of the most important founders of modern conservatism.

NOTES

1   Frank O'Gorman, *Edmund Burke: His Political Philosophy* (London: George Allen & Unwin, 1973), 11.

2   Edmund Burke, *A Vindication of Natural Society*, ed. Frank N. Pagano (Indianapolis, IN: Liberty Fund, 1982, first published 1756), 5.

3   Edmund Burke, "Letter to John Farr and John Harris, Esqrs, Sheriffs of the City of Bristol, on the Affairs of America, April 3, 1777," in *The Works of the Right Honourable Edmund Burke in Twelve Volumes, Volume the Second* (London: John C. Nimmo, 1887), 228.

4   Edmund Burke, "Speech of Edmund Burke, Esq., On Moving His Resolutions for Conciliation with the Colonies," in *Select Works of Edmund Burke*, vol. 1 (Indianapolis, IN: Liberty Fund, 1999), 143.

5   Burke, "Conciliation with the Colonies," 145.

6   Edmund Burke, "Speech in the Impeachment," in *The Works of Edmund Burke with a Memoir* (New York: George Dearborn, 1836), 302.

7   Burke, "Speech in the Impeachment," 302.

8   Frank M. Turner, "Edmund Burke: The Political Actor Thinking," Introduction to *Reflections on the Revolution in France*, ed. Frank M. Turner (New Haven, CT: Yale University Press, 2003), xxiii.

9   Edmund Burke, "Letters on a Regicide Peace," in *The Works of the Right Hon. Edmund Burke* (London: Henry G. Bohn, 1841), 315.

SECTION 3
IMPACT

MODULE 9
THE FIRST RESPONSES

KEY POINTS

- Many people responded to Reflections. Thomas Paine* tackled Burke head on by writing *Rights of Man*, his own theory of contemporary politics.

- Burke attacked Paine and his views in a written response titled *An Appeal from the New to the Old Whigs*.

- In the early days after the French Revolution* Burke was widely criticized in Britain. But after 1792, when the Revolution degenerated into The Terror,* he was suddenly hailed as a prophet.

Criticism

From the day it was published Edmund Burke's *Reflections on the Revolution in France* provoked passionate, widespread criticism. The debate was emotionally charged because supporters of Enlightenment-style* rationalism* believed the "abstract" theories they advanced to be self-evidently true, whereas Burke believed them to be self-evidently false. This argument set tradition against radicalism and went on to become one of the foundations of modern politics.

The pamphlet's first critic was Burke's fellow parliamentarian Lord James Mackintosh.* In a pamphlet entitled *Vindicae Gallicae,* Mackintosh wrote, "Mr. Burke has grounded his eloquent apology purely on [the aristocracy's] *individual* and *moral character.*" But Mackintosh believed the right approach was "their political and collective character."[1] Mackintosh felt that Burke needed to let go of his love for aristocracy and allow progress to happen.

> ❝ I am contending for the rights of the living, and against their being willed away and controlled and contracted for by the manuscript assumed authority of the dead, and Mr. Burke is contending for the authority of the dead over the rights and freedom of the living. ❞
>
> Thomas Paine, *The Rights of Man*

Most famously, *Reflections* inspired critical responses from the British-American political writer Thomas Paine in his book *Rights of Man* (1791).[2] In true Enlightenment style, he said: "Mr. Burke is contending for the authority of the dead over the rights and freedom of the living."[3]

The British philosopher Mary Wollstonecraft* also offered up her views in the works *A Vindication of the Rights of Men* (1790) and *A Vindication of the Rights of Woman* (1792). Outraged at what she saw as Burke's unfounded dismissal of natural rights,* Wollstonecraft wrote: "Will Mr. Burke be at the trouble to inform us, how far we are to go back to discover the rights of men, since the light of reason is such a fallacious guide that none but fools trust to its cold investigation?"[4] Wollstonecraft felt that the "rights of man" cannot be found in history because they are the victory of modern man over his oppression. Frustrated by Burke's emotive reaction to what she considers a beautiful moment in history, Wollstonecraft concludes he is too "pampered" and "emotional" to understand the glory of the French Revolution.

The debate did not change most people's views of the text. Burke was supported by people who were already pro-establishment and was rubbished by people who were already radical. The debate only seemed to make people stick to their positions even more.

Responses

Burke often refused to read things that were critical of him, because he said he was not likely to alter his own opinions. Similarly, he refused to engage in a dialogue because he knew he was unlikely to alter his critics' views.[5] Burke's most impassioned defense of his position came in his 1791 book *An Appeal from the New to the Old Whigs*. Burke was a member of the Whig* political party, but he found himself at odds with certain other important party members, especially Charles James Fox.* Fox supported the French Revolution and agreed with the views of Thomas Paine and Mary Wollstonecraft. Burke accuses this group of "subversion of nothing short of the whole constitution of this kingdom."[6] Burke felt that his critics dismissed the benefits of British government because of their zeal for abstract liberty. *An Appeal* is largely directed toward Fox. "Far from meriting the praises of a great genius like Mr. Fox [the Revolution] cannot be approved by any man of common sense."[7]

In *An Appeal* Burke restates his conclusion from *Reflections* that "the will of the people" is less important than the thousands of years of history that have shaped the state. He writes, "Our country is not a thing of mere physical locality whose government can be hired and fired at will." To Burke, the nation was "a duty" to past and future generations, "a social, civil relation" that ensures prosperity, even though we may not think every aspect is perfect.[8] In essence, Burke rejects the criticism that he is a lover of authority, as he was portrayed in political cartoons. He makes the case that even those who love republican liberty should not support politicians who support republican liberty, because ultimately those politicians cannot deliver an effective government.

Conflict and Consensus

The general opinion of Burke changed when Britain went to war with France in 1793. Suddenly he was seen as a prophet because his fears about the outcome of the French Revolution had been vindicated by the events of The Terror, where suspicion and mistrust led to thousands of politically motivated murders. In the nineteenth century Burke was remembered "as a model statesman" and the debate about the value of his collected works was continued in the literary sphere.[9] The English essayist William Hazlitt,* for example, valued the way Burke combined imaginative prose with political conclusions. In an 1819 essay called *The Character of Mr. Burke* Hazlitt wrote that the "union between the idea and the illustration gave animation and attraction to subjects in themselves barren of ornament, but which at the same time are pregnant with the most important consequences."[10]

Burke's continuing popularity shows how views of a thinker can change depending on circumstances. When *Reflections* came out in 1790 Burke was struggling to revive his political career. Initial reactions to it made it seem as if the work might finally sink that career. Instead, it made him famous forever.

NOTES

1   James Mackintosh, *Vindicae Gallicae* (Indianapolis, IN: Liberty Fund, 2006), 102.

2   Thomas Paine, *Rights of Man*, ed. Ronald Herder (Mineola, NY: Dover, 1999). First published in two parts, 1791–92.

3   Paine, *Rights*, 10.

4   Mary Wollstonecraft, *A Vindication of the Rights of Men, in a Letter to the Right Honourable Edmund Burke; Occasioned by His Reflections on the Revolution in France* (Charlottesville, VA: Intelex), 11.

5   F. P. Lock, *Edmund Burke: Volume II: 1784–1797* (Oxford: Oxford University Press, 2009), 351.

6   Edmund Burke, "An Appeal from the New to the Old Whigs," in *Further Reflections on the French Revolution*, ed. Daniel E. Ritchie, ch. 4 (Indianapolis, IN: Liberty Fund, 1992, first published 1790), 58.

7   Burke, *Appeal*, 63.

8   Burke, *Appeal*, 161.

9   Peter J. Stanlis, "Edmund Burke in the Twentieth Century," in *The Relevance of Edmund* Burke, ed. Peter J. Stanlis (New York: P.J. Kenedy, 1997), 27.

10 William Hazlitt, "Character of Mr. Burke, 1807," in *Hazlitt on English Literature: An Introduction to the Appreciation of Literature,* ed. Jacob Zeitlin (New York: Oxford University Press, 1913), 189.

THE EVOLVING DEBATE

KEY POINTS

- Burke's rejection of radical ideology has remained at the heart of conservative* thought in both literature and politics.

- The central themes of *Reflections*—the need to preserve existing institutions and reject radical, universal principles—are widely seen as providing the basis of conservatism.

- Burke's conservatism is still used today as a prototype for conservative politics. The journalist and notable conservative critic David Brooks* used *Reflections* to evaluate the USA's 2003 invasion of Iraq.

Uses and Problems

Reflections on the Revolution in France has had a lasting impact on political thought in the West by forming the basis of "traditionalist conservatism." It was Edmund Burke's rejection of ideology,* his dismissal of pure reason, and his disdain of liberalism* that placed him at the heart of conservative thought in nineteenth-century Britain and twentieth-century America.

Burke had a profound influence on non-political thinkers, including the British poet Samuel Taylor Coleridge,* but his lasting influences have been on politicians and political thinkers. The nineteenth-century Conservative—or Tory*—British Prime Minister Benjamin Disraeli* took Burke's ideas and put them into practice. This became known as "one-nation conservatism."* The name comes from Disraeli's famous "one-nation" speech in 1872 where he claimed the Tory Party had "Three great objects. The first is to maintain the

> ❝ The worlds of history and science, in spite of the testimonials to the completeness and perfection of their character with which they come before us, have turned out on examination to be abstract and defective ... And it is timed to consider ... the world of practical experience. ❞
>
> Michael Oakeshott, *Experience and its Modes*

institutions of the country, especially the monarchy ... The second ... is to uphold the Empire," and the third "the improvement of the condition of the people."[1] Disraeli acknowledges that "improving the condition of the people" means forcing politics into "questions of sewage." He also says that this is of prime importance. "The Palace is unsafe if the cottage is unhappy."[2] This is a very Burkean line of reasoning. The social orders are not being turned on their head for some abstract concept of justice, but aspects of social life are being adjusted to protect the institutions Britain already has.

British conservatives maintained this position throughout the twentieth century. One of Burke's biographers, Jesse Norman,* draws a strong connection between Burke's theories and those of twentieth-century British conservative thinker Michael Oakeshott.* Norman writes, "Oakeshott and Burke both offer a profound critique of the excessive claims of reason." According to Norman this challenges two parts of modern society: liberal socialism "with its belief in the guiding role of intellectuals in using the state to remodel society ... [and] the economic fundamentalism of über-libertarians* on the right."[3] Norman felt that Oakeshott's opinion that government is a complex beast and that we should not try to reduce any aspect of it to a single aim came directly from Burke's position. But Oakeshott distances himself from Burke. He sees Burke as a reactionary conservative and himself as a liberal.

Schools of Thought

Burke's core idea—that political change should be carried out in slow and steady increments rather than by revolutionary upheavals—resonated outside of Britain. The modern conservative movement in the United States has been profoundly influenced by Burke's ideas. American twentieth-century conservative political scientist Samuel P. Huntington* states that Burke's argument defined the core concern of conservatism as a political idea, both through history and in the present day. Huntington wrote, "In any society, there may be institutions to be conserved, but there are never conservative institutions."[4] In other words, conservatism shuns universal principles. Instead, it looks to preserve the institutions that exist in society thanks to history, nature, and previous generations, and that best provide for that society's needs. This idea, referred to by Huntington as "Burkean," crystallized into a political position throughout the West in the nineteenth and twentieth centuries. These concepts include the claim that, as Huntington said, "society is a natural, organic product of slow historical growth"; a presumption in favor of existing over new institutions and a distrust of pure theory.[5]

The American political theorist Russell Kirk* wrote that *Reflections* was the first work of "conscious conservatism, in the modern sense." This sensibility was behind Burke's theory emphasizing the importance of "preservation of the ancient moral traditions of humanity."[6] This includes an assumption that there is a natural law, or some fixed idea of what is moral, an appreciation that society requires inequality and social classes, and a distrust of speedy reform.

In Current Scholarship

Other modern thinkers who identify with Burke include the German-American political philosopher Leo Strauss* and the American academic Peter J. Stanlis. Both quoted Burke heavily in their writing on natural law theory* as it applies to conservatism:

Strauss in *Natural Right and History* and Stanlis in *Edmund Burke and the Natural Law*.[7] Natural law theory sets out that certain aspects of human society are "natural," and cannot be reasoned or improved upon, unless the improvement makes them more in accordance with nature.

Burke's "natural law" argument stemmed from his belief that man was a social animal and therefore the laws and arrangements of society are the laws of nature. Modern conservative thinkers, such as Strauss and Stanlis, agree that Burke's natural law theory is a useful defense against positivism* (looking for truth through science), totalitarianism* (the government of one unchecked ruler), and popular tyranny (the absolute abuse of authority). Burke's thought, they suggest, "represents a visible return to a better past."[8] Burke argued this position against Enlightenment* thinkers who put forward their theory of "natural rights." Stanlis wrote that Burke's cautiousness was among the most important aspects of his natural law theory: "Prudence was for Burke not an intellectual, but a moral virtue, and as such … the best positive alternative to the errors of metaphysical abstraction."[9] Stanlis considered Burke's prudence to be the best safeguard of the natural law in society. To Burke, and those inspired by him, society was like a plant that needed to tended, cared for, and nurtured. To cut into it to study it in the hope of improving future plants would be a catastrophe.

NOTES

1 Benjamin Disraeli, quoted in Richard Carr, *One Nation Britain: History and the Progressive Tradition, and Practical Ideas for Today's Politicians* (Farnham: Ashgate, 2014), 26.

2 Disraeli, in Carr, *One Nation*, 26.

3 Jesse Norman, "Burke, Oakeshott, and the Intellectual Roots of Modern Conservatism," Oakeshott Memorial Lecture delivered at the London School of Economics, November 12, 2013, accessed November 24, 2014, www.jesse4hereford.com/pdf/LSE_Lecture_Burke_and_Oakeshott.pdf.

4   Samuel P. Huntington, "Conservatism as Ideology," *American Political Science Review* 51, no. 2 (1957): 458.

5   Huntington, "Conservatism as Ideology," 456.

6   Russell Kirk, *The Conservative Mind: Burke to Eliot* (Washington, D.C.: Eagle Publishing, 2001), 6, 8.

7   Peter J. Stanlis, *Edmund Burke and the Natural Law* (Piscataway, NJ: Transaction, 2003).

8   Harvey Mansfield, "Burke's Conservatism," in *An Imaginative Whig: Rethinking the Life and Thought of Edmund Burke* (Columbia, MO: University of Missouri Press, 2005), 60.

9   Peter J. Stanlis, "The Basis of Burke's Political Conservatism," *Modern Age* 5, no. 3 (1961): 266.

MODULE 11
IMPACT AND INFLUENCE TODAY

KEY POINTS

- Burke's *Reflections* is still relevant as a foundational text in modern conservatism* and is still used to criticize ideas that are based on abstract reason and ideology.*

- *Reflections* is still used by skeptical thinkers such as British philosopher and politician Baroness Onora O'Neill* to argue that universal international human rights are dangerously vague.

- Supporters of human rights say that Burke's theories were not meant to be guides to policy. Indian economist and philosopher Amartya Sen* argues human rights are an aspiration.

Position

Reflections on the Revolution in France by Edmund Burke is still useful to policy makers today. The Austrian economist Friedrich von Hayek* applies the same principles as Burke. In his 1944 book *The Road to Serfdom*, Hayek talks of the need for measured, organic growth and for a distrust of abstract theory. He says that it was the inability to follow these principles that led to the mass failure of planned economies in the twentieth century. Hayek wrote, "The enthusiasm for 'organization' of everything and … inability to leave anything to the simple power of organic growth"[1] leads to disastrous consequences—totalitarianism.* He argues that tyrants need only mention "philosophy, light, liberality [and] the Rights of Men" to justify crimes against their subjects.[2]

This is why, as Peter J. Stanlis* said, *Reflections* still has a "special significance to twentieth century man." He said the text is "Burke's

> ❝ Most conservatives adopt conservative ideas in order to defend one particular established order. In this respect their conservatism is instrumental rather than primary. Burke, however, was the conservative archetype because his impulse was to defend all existing institutions wherever located and however challenged. ❞
>
> Samuel P. Huntington, "Conservatism as an Ideology"

reply to the totalitarian doctrines of the French Revolution."[3] On the surface this may seem like an unusual claim. After all, the French Revolution* was concerned with overthrowing an autocratic* king, and its slogan was "*liberté, egalité, fraternité*" ("liberty, equality, brotherhood"). On the surface none of these revolutionary aims seem totalitarian. However, in pursuit of these abstract principles the revolutionary government seized total power. It wanted to create a utopia—a perfect state—and in so doing it committed monstrous crimes. This idea had great power in America during the Cold War* of the second half of the twentieth century, because the same criticism could be applied to the Soviet Union.*

The American diplomat and political scientist George Kennan* wrote that "freedom" cannot be found by those who look for it by setting up societies "so vast and complicated that the individual can no longer sense or survey his relation to the whole." Kennan continued that totalitarianism can happen when all-encompassing social change is made looking for some better *theoretical* life.[4] To Kennan, the Soviet Union was a totalitarian state designed to enforce a utopia that is intellectually attractive, but so removed from the experience of everyday life that people do not understand it. Freedom, says Kennan, must be sought through "the wisdom of the ages, and in the ethical codes that the great religions of civilizations have developed."[5] While the intention was to create a workers' paradise, the Soviet Union ended up costing tens of millions of lives in purges (especially The Great Purge*) and labor camps.* The way Burke and his *Reflections* foresaw much of this this is what gave the work such lasting impact. It confronts the problem of social organization by theory and resonates beyond its place and its time.

Interaction

Reflections has also gained contemporary relevance in the arena of International Relations. The book is regularly cited in debates about international human rights. Many critics argue that human rights are actually just Western rights, rooted to Western societies, and that they are not universal at all. American academic Irene Oh* writes, "Declaring as a human right conditions of marriage imparts the flavor to human rights overall as a project of Western cultural imperialism."[6] By this Oh means that some cultures may have different views on marriage and so they do not see a "universal" declaration of human rights as belonging in their own society.

Perhaps the most famous modern human rights commentator to quote Burke is Baroness Onora O'Neill. She opens her article "The Dark Side of Human Rights" with a quotation from Burke: "What is the use of discussing a man's abstract right to food or medicine … The question is upon the method of procuring and administering them."[7] O'Neill is referring to the language of the United Nations Universal Declaration of Human Rights. The Declaration begins: "everyone is entitled to all the rights and freedoms set forth in this Declaration, without distinction of any kind," including "political, jurisdictional, or international status."[8] These include rights to take part in the political process, the right to work, and the right to an adequate standard of living and education. O'Neill's paper points out that while these rights may seem attractive, what she terms the "international human rights culture" is not without problems. It is, she writes, "replete with claims about abstract rights to goods and services [such as food and medicine]," which are "often muddled or vague."[9] Attempting to legislate according to these rights can produce inconsistent results. Society is very complicated, but these rights are very simple and well defined. O'Neill argues that proposing lofty goals, but not answering questions of how best to achieve them, actually damages the human rights agenda.

The Continuing Debate

The Indian economist Amartya Sen addressed O'Neill's challenge that human rights are too vague to legislate in an article entitled "Elements of a Theory of Human Rights." Sen's core concern was to show that human rights theories are "primarily ethical demands." They are not necessarily calls for legislation in societies where they may not fit. Sen wrote that the call for rights generates "reasons for action for agents who are in a position to help in the promoting or safeguarding of the underlying freedoms."[10] So, Sen moderated the claims of universal human rights saying they should be taken not as literal instructions, but as inspiration for lawmakers in particular contexts to adapt them as they see fit.

Some supporters of human rights, such as American political theorist John Ikenberry,* argue that human rights based on Western systems *can* be universal. Ikenberry wrote: "Even though liberal democracy* and democratic capitalism* did emerge in the West, [human rights] are not uniquely or essentially Western." And even though they are "imagined," they are still morally persuasive. Ikenberry's argument is that it does not matter how much someone identifies with a "universal" human right, or with its Western origin, because they are beneficial whatever context they are applied in.

NOTES

1   Friedrich A. von Hayek, *The Road to Serfdom*, 50th anniversary edition (Chicago, IL: University of Chicago Press, 1994), 200.

2   Edmund Burke, *Reflections on the Revolution in France*, ed. with an Introduction and Notes by L. G. Mitchell, Oxford World's Classics (Oxford: Oxford University Press, 1993 and 2009), 116.

3   Peter J. Stanlis, "Edmund Burke in the Twentieth Century," in *The Relevance of Edmund* Burke, ed. Peter J. Stanlis (Washington, D.C.: Georgetown University Press, 1997), 45.

4   George Kennan, "Totalitarianism in the Modern World," in *Totalitarianism: Proceedings of a Conference Held at the American Academy of Arts and Sciences*, ed. Carl Friedrich (Cambridge, MA: Harvard University Press, 1954), 26.

5   Kennan, "Totalitarianism," 30–1.

6   Irene Oh, *The Rights of God: Islam, Human Rights, and Comparative Ethics*, (Washington, D.C.: Georgetown University Press, 2007), 32.

7   Onora O'Neill, "The Dark Side of Human Rights," *International Affairs* 81, no. 2 (2005): 427.

8   United Nations, *Universal Declaration of Human Rights*, accessed January 14, 2015, www.un.org/en/documents/udhr/.

9   Onora O'Neill, "The Dark Side of Human Rights," *International Affairs* 81, no. 2 (2005): 427.

10 Amartya Sen, "Elements of a Theory of Human Rights," *Philosophy and Public Affairs* 32, no. 4 (2004): 319.

WHERE NEXT?

KEY POINTS

- Contemporary conservatism* has disconnected with *Reflections*. Neoconservatism* is concerned with promoting democratic and free-market institutions around the world.

- *Reflections* will continue to be talked about by skeptics of all political views.

- *Reflections* remains significant as a Counter-Enlightenment* historical text. It is still relevant because it rejects the idea of ideology* in general, even if it is not directly applicable to individual policies.

Potential

Edmund Burke's *Reflections on the Revolution in France* has lost some of its relevance to contemporary American politics, because Burke's form of "traditionalist" conservatism has been eclipsed by neoconservatism. Neoconservatism is an ideology, rather than a method. As Samuel P. Huntington said, "there may be institutions to be conserved, but there are never conservative institutions."[1] But neoconservatism has universal ideological commitments. The American journalist and prominent neoconservative thinker Irving Kristol* writes: "Though there is much fancy rhetoric … about 'the purpose of American foreign policy,' there is really nothing [complicated] about this purpose."[2]

> **❝** What is extraordinary about Burke is his capacity for prophecy. That comes out of three things: first is his idea of history and the potential threat to the social order. The second is the deep understanding he has of human change, of human personality and of human nature. The third is a very nuanced and detailed grasp of the specific circumstances behind particular changes. **❞**
>
> Jesse Norman, "Edmund Burke, Our Chief of Men," *The Spectator*

Kristol says the United States has three priorities. These are as follows.

- "To ensure its national security as against the other great powers.
- [To encourage] other nations, especially the smaller ones, to mold their own social, political and economic institutions along lines familiar to the US.
- [To minimize] the possibility of naked armed conflict."[3]

It is the second point that is most problematic for followers of Burke. Neoconservatism thinks the American system is self-evidently the best and wants to reproduce it around the world. Kristol goes further in saying, "there is no superior, authoritative information available about the good life or the true nature of human happiness."[4] Neoconservatism believes the American system should be replicated precisely because it "liberates" people from directions. And that is the exact opposite of Burke's position.

Future Directions

Despite the rise of neoconservatism, Burke's analysis has not been entirely forgotten and *Reflections* will continue to be quoted and referred to by skeptics of all political views. In recent years political commentators have begun using Burke's writing to criticize neoconservative policies. In a 2007 article for *The New York Times*, entitled "The Republican Collapse," conservative intellectual David Brooks* criticized American conservatives for evoking Burkean ideas, but then failing to act on them. Brooks points to the Iraq War* as an example of the declining influence of Burke's ideals in the American political right. Brooks writes, "The Bush* administration has operated on the assumption that if you change the political institutions in Iraq, the society will follow. But the Burkean conservative believes that society is an organism … and that successful government institutions grow gradually from each nation's unique network of moral and social restraints."

Brooks says that the radical libertarian* streak in conservatism sees government as a threat to freedom. But the Burkean conservative "believes government is like fire—useful when used legitimately, but dangerous when not."[5] This suggests Burke's work has lost relevance as a guide to policy because, as Brooks argues, modern conservatives pursue such ideas as the free market or individual liberty as an ideology. However, they do this at the expense of the pragmatic* decision-making Burke favored. *Reflections* is likely to continue to be relevant as an example of an "ideal type" of pragmatic conservatism. So Burke's status will continue to make the ideas in *Reflections* central to modern political debates, even if they are no longer directly applicable to political policy.

Summary

Reflections is widely acknowledged as the founding work of modern conservatism. The French Revolution* has been heralded as the birth of modern political liberalism* and *Reflections* was its first major conservative examination. Burke's writing has remained a cautionary voice for all those who plan to radically reshape society, just as the French revolutionaries did in 1790. Their plan was devised out of an unproven liberal idea based on pure philosophy, even if it might have appeared intellectually attractive. As Burke wrote, "I should therefore suspend my congratulations on the new liberty of France, until I was informed how it had been combined with government, with public force, with the discipline and obedience of armies, with the collection of an effective and well distributed revenue, with morality and religion, with solidity and property, with peace and order, with civil and social manners."[6]

The ideas in *Reflections* have stood the test of time, but the thing that makes it unique is the way it predicted the future. In 1790 Burke wrote that the formation of a government in France based on abstract principles would result in disaster, and he said this two years before the French Revolution descended into the political violence known as The Terror* in late 1792. The criticisms made in *Reflections* work as a reminder that any government with an ambitious political project is not merely an experiment, but "a contrivance of human wisdom to provide for human wants."[7] Burke's criticism of radical politics addresses the ever-present temptation to strive for perfect political institutions along intellectually appealing lines. *Reflections* shows that this is dangerous when put into practice.

NOTES

1   Samuel P. Huntington, "Conservatism as Ideology," *American Political Science Review* 51, no. 2 (1957): 458.

2   Irving Kristol, *Neoconservatism: The Autobiography of an Idea* (New York: Simon & Schuster, 1995), 90.

3   Kristol, *Neoconservatism*, 90.

4   Kristol, *Neoconservatism*, 96.

5   David Brooks, "The Republican Collapse," *New York Times*, October 5, 2007, accessed October 1, 2013, www.nytimes.com/2007/10/05/opinion/05brooks.html?_r=0.

6   Edmund Burke, *Reflections on the Revolution in France*, ed. with an Introduction and Notes by L. G. Mitchell, Oxford World's Classics (Oxford:

GLOSSARY

GLOSSARY OF TERMS

American Revolution (1775–83): a period of political and military conflict in what would become the United States of America, as the inhabitants of Great Britain's 13 North American colonies overthrew the colonial government and British rule. Also called the US War of Independence or American Revolutionary War.

Ancien régime: from the French for "old regime," this was the political, religious, and social system of France from the fifteenth century until the late eighteenth century. The system was based on the entrenched class system and the authority of the Catholic Church.

Archetype: a typical example of a person or thing.

Aristocracy: the upper class of society; the aristocracy is generally made up of those with hereditary titles.

Autocracy: a government in which one person rules with absolute power.

British Empire (sixteenth–twentieth century): the total area ruled by England and then the United Kingdom. It was the largest empire in history, and covered 25 per cent of the world's total land area at its height.

Capitalism: an economic system based on private ownership, private enterprise, and the maximization of profit.

Catholic Church (or Roman Catholic Church): one of the major branches of the Christian religion. Its hierarchical structure has the Pope at its head.

Chivalry: a medieval knightly system with its own moral code.

Church of Ireland: is an Anglican Church representing the whole of Ireland that is broadly Protestant in outlook but accepts some Catholic patterns of worship while rejecting the authority of the Pope.

Cold War (1946–89): a period of tension between America and the Soviet Union. While the two countries never engaged in direct military conflict, they engaged in covert and proxy wars and espionage against one another.

Conservatism: a political philosophy that promotes a return to traditional moral values and the defense of existing institutions.

Constitution: a body of principles and laws that are used as the basis for governing a country, state, or organization.

Counter-Enlightenment: a term used by the twentieth-century Russian-British philosopher Isaiah Berlin to bring together all the thinkers who were against the Enlightenment.

Declaration of Right (1688): an English legal document that instituted 13 legal limitations on the power of the monarchy, especially with regard to taxes and protection of property.

Democracy: a form of government where citizens elect a body of representatives who will then act in their name.

Divine Right of Kings: the idea that royal authority in a given land is given to the king by God, so to disobey the king is also to disobey God.

The Enlightenment (seventeenth and eighteenth centuries): a period of European intellectual history that emphasized reason and anti-traditionalism based on the scientific method.

Entailment: a legal term that makes the inheritance of an estate conditional on its not being sold or altered in some way. Burke means the term to suggest that England inherited its constitution on the condition that it be preserved.

French Revolution (1789–99): a decade of intense political upheaval in France where revolutionaries experimented with a number of different regimes—a constitutional monarchy, a revolutionary dictatorship, a popular direct democracy, a liberal republic—before ending with the military dictatorship of Napoleon Bonaparte.

Glorious Revolution (1688): the name commonly given to the overthrow of the Roman Catholic English King James II by an alliance of Parliamentarians and the Dutch ruler William of Orange, who subsequently became William III of Great Britain, ruling jointly with his wife, Mary II, who was the daughter of James II.

Government by consent: a principle of popular sovereignty, which states that rulers are only made legitimate if the ruled agree to the nature, duration, and form of rule.

The Great Purge (1936–40): a period of state violence and political repression in the former Soviet Union, where hundreds of thousands of people were executed or imprisoned as perceived threats to the government.

Hubris: over-confidence or extreme pride.

Ideology: a system of ideas and ideals, often forming the roots of an economic or political theory.

Imagery: figurative language used in works of literature that helps conjure a picture in people's minds.

Imperialism: the process of extending a country's power and influence in other countries through colonization.

Industrial Revolution (eighteenth and nineteenth centuries): a major advance in technology for manufacturing industry, where machines and steam power allowed mass production. It began in Britain before spreading quickly to Western Europe and North America.

Inflation: a set of circumstances that causes an increase in prices and a decrease in the value of money.

Iraq War (2003–11): fought between the United States and Iraq in two phases. The first was a conventional war against Saddam Hussein's government, while the second was a prolonged occupation that consisted of state-building efforts on the part of the Americans.

Labor camp: a kind of prison in which prisoners are forced to work.

Liberal Party (1859–1988): a political party in the United Kingdom comprised of several parties (including the Whigs, the Radicals, and the Peelites). Notably, they introduced a number of reforms that created the British "welfare state."

Liberalism: a political philosophy founded on ideas concerned with individual freedom and equality.

Libertarianism: an extremely "hands off" political view that believes in only the lightest state intervention in the lives of its people.

Magna Charta (1215): a legal document enshrining the legal duties of the king towards some of his subjects. It has been considered by some to be the "constitution" of England, establishing "rule of law" over the power of the monarchy.

Metaphor: a figure of speech in which a word or phrase is used as a symbol for something else.

Metaphysics: an area of philosophy that looks to explain the nature of being and the world around it.

Monarchy: a state led by a sovereign head, which could be a king or a queen, for example.

National Assembly (June–July 1789): an assembly formed of the commoners in parliament ("the Third Estate") that seized power from the rest of the organs of the French state in June 1789. It was replaced by the Legislative Assembly in October 1791, which attempted to create a new state out of what the National Assembly seized.

Natural law theory: the belief that human interaction is governed by innate laws. Natural law theory holds that positive law (the law that is written down) should reflect this "natural law" as closely as possible.

Natural rights theory: asserts that all humanity possesses a number of rights that do not flow from any institution or law, but from nature itself. These rights are "inalienable," so cannot be denied.

Neoconservatism: American political movement that emphasizes proactive promotion of free markets and individual liberty around the world.

"One-nation conservatism": a British conservative ideology associated with a picture of society as interdependent. For example, the lower classes depend on the leadership of the upper class, who depends on the labor of the lower class.

Parliament: the supreme legal authority in the United Kingdom, which can create or end any law. It is made up of the House of Commons, the House of Lords, and the sovereign.

Popular sovereignty: the idea that the authority to govern a country is based on the consent of the people.

Positivism: a philosophy of science that prizes scientific verification as a means for discovering what is true.

Pragmatism: a way of dealing with problems sensibly and realistically using practical considerations rather than abstract ideas and theories.

Proselytize: the act of trying to convert someone to a religious point of view.

Protestantism: a Christian Church that separated from the Roman Catholic Church after the sixteenth-century Reformation. It includes the Baptist, Presbyterian, and Lutheran Churches.

Quakerism (also called the Religious Society of Friends): a sect of Christianity formed in seventeenth-century England that emphasizes pacifism and charity.

Quarantine: isolation where people or animals are held, often in relation to a fear of the spread of disease.

Radicalism: behavior that rejects tradition and favors extreme changes, particularly in politics.

Rationalism: a belief system that truth can be obtained through the application of thought. It is contrasted with empiricism, which holds that truth is only knowable by experience.

Reactionary: a point of view or position that is against either reform, or political or social progress.

Revolution Society (1788–92): a London club formed to commemorate the Glorious Revolution of 1688 and which provided vocal support for the French Revolution.

Rhetoric: Persuasive writing or speaking, designed to convince of a particular point of view.

Soviet Union (1922–91): a communist union of states administered in Moscow, Russia. At the end of the Cold War the Soviet Union dissolved and many states adopted capitalism.

State of nature: a theoretical idea used by some social contract theorists to depict life before society existed and to illustrate why humans would inevitably enter into a social contract.

Supply and demand: a "law" in economics. Increases in demand of a good or service lead to increased prices, and therefore increases in supply of that good or service then reduce prices.

The Terror: also known as the Reign of Terror, this was a period of political violence in France between late 1792 and 1794 where mass executions were carried out by the French revolutionary government.

Theocracy: a system of government where religious people rule in the name of a god.

Toryism: a British political philosophy combining traditionalism and conservatism. The Tory political faction emerged after the English Civil War (1642–51). "Tory" is the nickname given to the modern Conservative Party in Britain and many of her former colonies.

Totalitarianism: a form of government that is highly centralized in one ruler who is unrestricted by a constitution or checks and balances.

Universal rights: entitlements to things (such as life or freedom) to which all people are thought to be entitled, simply on the basis that they are human.

Utopia: a place, state, or condition that is considered perfect in all ways.

Whig Party (1678–1868): a political party in the Parliament of Great Britain. Whigs believed in parliamentary supremacy over the monarch and a liberal economic program.

PEOPLE MENTIONED IN THE TEXT

Marie Antoinette (1755–93) was an Austrian noblewoman and became Queen of France on her marriage to King Louis XVI at the age of 14 in 1770. She was famously executed in the aftermath of the French Revolution.

James R. Arnold is an American military historian. He specializes in the Napoleonic and Civil Wars.

Walter Bagehot (1826–77) was a British political thinker, industrialist, and public intellectual. Famously, he was editor-in-chief of *The Economist*, and wrote extensively on the English constitution and banking industry.

Norman P. Barry (1944–2008) was a British political philosopher and professor of social and political theory at the University of Buckingham.

Isaiah Berlin (1909–97) was a Russian-British philosopher and political thinker. His most famous work was on the concept of liberty, drawing a line between "negative liberty" (what we are free to do without interference) and "positive liberty" (what we are enabled to do with help).

David Brooks (born 1961) is an American conservative journalist who contributes regularly to the *New York Times*.

George W. Bush (born 1946) was the 43rd President of the United States from 2001 to 2009.

Marcus Tullius Cicero (106 BCE–43 BCE) was an ancient Roman jurist, politician, and political thinker. He was a proponent of republican government, and believed in the government's ability to deliver justice.

Samuel Taylor Coleridge (1772–1834) was a famous English poet, critic, and philosopher.

Charles-Jean-François Depont (1767–97) was a young French nobleman with whom Burke corresponded. He was a member of the National Assembly.

Benjamin Disraeli (1804–81) was a British prime minister who engaged in the first modern election campaign and presided over significant expansion of the British Empire.

Henry Dundas, 1st Viscount Melville, Baron Dunira (1742–1811) was a Scottish Tory politician. He held office as Secretary of State for War from 1791 to 1794.

Charles James Fox (1749–1806) was a British Whig politician and party leader. Fox famously disagreed with Burke's *Reflections*, believing the French Revolution to be a good thing.

Milton Friedman (1912–2006) was an American economist associated with the Chicago School of economic thought; he won the 1998 Nobel Memorial Prize in Economic Sciences. His most famous argument was that the government cannot "print money" to create economic prosperity in the long term.

Norman Hampson (1922–2011) was a British historian. He was a specialist in French History and was first President of the Society for the Study of French History.

Warren Hastings (1732–1818) was a British colonial statesman. He was made Governor-General of Bengal, ruling the British possessions in India from 1773 to 1785. He was accused of corruption by Edmund Burke, and the trial dragged on for seven years before he was finally acquitted.

Friedrich von Hayek (1899–1992) was an Austrian economist who worked primarily in Britain. He is most famous for his analysis of the interdependence of economic and social phenomena.

William Hazlitt (1788–1830) was a Romantic English writer and essayist, famous for his critical work on art, drama, and philosophy. He remains one of the greatest critics in the English language.

Thomas Hobbes (1588–1679) was an English political thinker. His most famous book, *Leviathan*, argued that a strong state was necessary in order to protect the interests of the governed.

Samuel P. Huntington (1927–2008) was an American conservative political scientist, famous for his book *The Clash of Civilizations and the Remaking of World Order*.

John Ikenberry (born 1954) is an American political theorist and academic. He is Professor of Politics and International Affairs at Princeton University and is in favor of a rule-based international order. He is considered the premier thinker on liberal internationalism.

King James II (1633–1701) was King of England and Ireland. As he was a Roman Catholic his rule was controversial and culminated in the Glorious Revolution of 1688.

George Kennan (1904–2005) was an American diplomat and political scientist. He was a key figure in the Cold War, best known for advocating a policy of "containment," which represented active attempts to reduce Soviet influence.

Russell Kirk (1918–94) was a conservative American political theorist. His 1953 book *The Conservative Mind: From Burke to Eliot* is considered to be very important.

Irving Kristol (1920–2009) was an American journalist and political commentator who is considered to be the founder of neoconservatism.

F. P. Lock (born 1948) is a Canadian English professor and a prominent biographer of Edmund Burke.

John Locke (1632–1704) was an English philosopher famous as one of the founders of classical liberalism, in which the freedom of the individual is emphasized and the power of the government is limited.

James Mackintosh (1765–1832) was a Scottish politician and philosopher who advocated liberal causes. He wrote *Vindicae Gallicae: Defence of the French Revolution and its English Admirers, Against the Accusations of the Right Hon. Edmund Burke* in response to *Reflections* and was considered by Burke to be his best critic.

Joseph de Maistre (1753–1821) was a French philosopher and nobleman. He argued that the monarchy and all the structures of society were divinely given and above human intervention.

Charles-Louis de Secondat, Baron de La Brède et de Montesquieu (1689–1755) was a French political thinker, public figure, and member of the aristocracy. His *Spirit of the Laws* is a seminal argument for (among other things) constitutional government, the abolition of slavery, and the importance of setting laws in historical context.

Sylvia Neely is an American historian. She specializes in comparative history of the French Revolution.

Jesse Norman (born 1962) is a British Conservative Member of Parliament and biographer of Edmund Burke.

Michael Oakeshott (1901–90) was a British political thinker. He was most interested in the philosophy of history, but his experience-based approach also made him an important conservative philosopher.

Frank O'Gorman is Emeritus Professor of History at the University of Manchester, specializing in eighteenth-century British history and conservatism.

Irene Oh is an American academic in religious studies. She is primarily concerned with comparing ethical approaches across cultures.

Baroness Onora O'Neill of Bengarve (born 1941) is a prominent Northern Irish philosopher politician who currently chairs the Equality and Human Rights Commission.

Thomas Paine (1737–1809) was a British-American political activist and author. He was an advocate for American independence from Britain with the publication of *Common Sense* (1776) and for the French Revolution with the publication of *Rights of Man* (1791–92).

Richard Price (1723–91) was a Welsh political philosopher, dissenting preacher, and active pro-revolutionary liberal political figure in England.

Amartya Sen (born 1933) is an Indian economist, philosopher, and recipient of the 1998 Nobel Memorial Prize in Economic Sciences.

Abbé Sieyès, Emmanuel Joseph Sieyès (1748–1836) was a French religious figure and political thinker. He is widely considered to be the unofficial theorist of the French Revolution and was heavily involved in the rise of Napoleon Bonaparte.

Adam Smith (1723–90) was a Scottish moral and political philosopher. He is widely considered to be the founding father of modern economics with his 1776 book *The Wealth of Nations.*

Peter J. Stanlis (1919–2011) was an American academic in politics and history and a professor of humanities at Rockford College. He was notably the leading authority on Burke. His book *Edmund Burke and the Natural Law* was published in 1958.

Leo Strauss (1899–1973) was an American political theorist known for his work on classical political philosophy. Strauss famously influenced the conservative movement.

Frank M. Turner (1944–2010) was a distinguished American intellectual historian and Provost of Yale University. He was primarily a historian of ideas and was especially interested in the evolution of the idea of "the West" as an entity.

Charles Watson-Wentworth, 2nd Marquess of Rockingham (1730–82) was a British statesman, leader of the Whig party, and Prime Minister of the United Kingdom.

King William III of England (1650–1702) was a Dutch "stadtholder" (meaning head of state) who fought several successful wars on behalf of Protestants in Europe. He was made King of England in 1689 in the aftermath of the Glorious Revolution of 1688.

Mary Wollstonecraft (1759–97) was a British philosopher and early advocate of women's rights. Her works *A Vindication of the Rights of Men* (1790) and *A Vindication of the Rights of Woman* (1792) are considered very important works.

WORKS CITED

WORKS CITED

Arnold, James R. *The Aftermath of the French Revolution*. Minneapolis, MN: Twenty-First Century Books, 2009.

Barry, Norman P. "The Political Economy of Edmund Burke." In *Edmund Burke: His Life and Legacy*, edited by Ian Crowe, 104–14. Dublin: Four Courts Press, 1997.

Berlin, Isaiah. "Joseph de Maistre and the Origins of Fascism." In *The Crooked Timber of Humanity; Chapters in the History of Ideas*, edited by Henry Hardy. Princeton, NJ: Princeton University Press, 2013.

Brooks, David. "The Republican Collapse." *New York Times*, October 5, 2007. Accessed October 1, 2013. www.nytimes.com/2007/10/05/opinion/05brooks. html?_r=0.

Burke, Edmund. "An Appeal from the New to the Old Whigs." In *Further Reflections on the French Revolution*, edited by Daniel E. Ritchie, ch. 4. Indianapolis, IN: Liberty Fund, 1992, first published 1790.

"An Essay Towards an Abridgement of the English History." In *The Works of the Right Honourable Edmund Burke in Twelve Volumes, Volume the Seventh*, 159–89. London: John C. Nimmo, 1887.

"Letter to John Farr and John Harris, Esqrs, Sheriffs of the City of Bristol, on the Affairs of America, April 3, 1777." In *The Works of the Right Honourable Edmund Burke in Twelve Volumes, Volume the Second*, 187–246. London: John C. Nimmo, 1887.

"Letters on a Regicide Peace." In *The Works of the Right Hon. Edmund Burke*. London: Henry G. Bohn, 1848.

Reflections on the Revolution in France. Edited with an Introduction and Notes by L. G. Mitchell, Oxford World's Classics (Oxford: Oxford University Press, 1993 and 2009).

"Speech of Edmund Burke, Esq., On Moving His Resolutions for Conciliation with the Colonies." In *Select Works of Edmund Burke*, vol. 1. Indianapolis, IN: Liberty Fund, 1999.

"Speech in the Impeachment." In *The Works of Edmund Burke with a Memoir*. New York: George Dearborn, 1836.

"Thoughts on French Affairs." In *The Works of the Right Honourable Edmund Burke in Twelve Volumes, Volume the Fourth*, 313–78. London: John C. Nimmo, 1887.

A Vindication of Natural Society: Or, A View of the Miseries and Evils Arising to Mankind from Every Species of Artificial Society. Edited by Frank N. Pagano. Indianapolis, IN: Liberty Fund, 1982, first published 1756.

Campbell, Heather M. *The Britannica Guide to Political and Social Movements that Changed the Modern World*. New York: Britannica Educational Publishing, 2010.

Carr, Richard. *One Nation Britain: History, the Progressive Tradition, and Practical Ideas for Today's Politicians*. Farnham: Ashgate, 2014.

Hampson, Norman. *The Enlightenment*: *An Evaluation of its Assumptions, Attitudes and Values*. London: Penguin, 1990.

Hayek, Friedrich A. von. *The Road to Serfdom*, 50th anniversary edition. Chicago, IL: University of Chicago Press, 1994.

Hazlitt, William. "The Character of Mr. Burke." In *Hazlitt on English Literature*, compiled by Jacob Zeitlin, 172–91. New York: Oxford University Press, 1913.

Hobbes, Thomas. *Leviathan*. Edited with an Introduction and Notes by J. C. A. Gaskin. Oxford: Oxford University Press, 1998.

Huntington, Samuel P. "Conservatism as Ideology." *American Political Science Review* 51, no. 2 (1957): 454–73.

Insole, Christopher J. "Burke and the Natural Law." In *The Cambridge Companion to Edmund Burke*, edited by David Dwan and Christopher J. Insole, 117–30. Cambridge: Cambridge University Press, 2012.

James, Robert Rhodes. "The Relevance of Edmund Burke." In *Edmund Burke: His Life and Legacy*, edited by Ian Crowe. Dublin: Four Courts Press, 1997.

Kennan, George. "Totalitarianism in the Modern World." In *Totalitarianism: Proceedings of a Conference Held at the American Academy of Arts and Sciences*, edited by Carl Friedrich. Cambridge, MA: Harvard University Press, 1954.

Kirk, Russell. *The Conservative Mind: From Burke to Eliot*. Washington, D.C.: Regnery Publishing, 2001.

Kristol, Irving. *Neoconservatism: The Autobiography of an Idea*. New York: Free Press, 1995.

Lock, F. P. *Edmund Burke: Volume II: 1784–1797*. Oxford: Oxford University Press, 2009.

Locke, John, "Of Civil Government. Book II: The Second Treatise." In *Two Treatises of Government and a Letter Concerning Toleration*, edited by Ian Shapiro. New Haven, CT: Yale University Press, 2003

Mackintosh, James. *Vindicae Gallicae*. Indianapolis, IN: Liberty Fund, 2006.

de Maistre, Joseph. "Against Rousseau." In *The Collected Works of Joseph de Maistre*, edited and annotated by Richard Lebrun. Charlottesville, VA: Intelex, 2008.

Mansfield, Harvey. "Burke's Conservatism." In *An Imaginative Whig: Rethinking the Life and Thought of Edmund Burke*, edited by Ian Crowe, 59–70. Columbia, MO: University of Missouri Press, 2005.

Montesquieu, Charles de. *The Spirit of the Laws*. Edited by Anne M. Cohler, Basia C. Miller, and Harold S. Stone. Cambridge: Cambridge University Press, 1989,

Neely, Sylvia. *A Concise History of the French Revolution*. Lanham, MD: Rowman & Littlefield, 2008.

Norman, Jesse. "Burke, Oakeshott, and the Intellectual Roots of Modern Conservatism." Oakeshott Memorial Lecture delivered at the London School of Economics, November 12, 2013. Accessed November 24, 2014. www.jesse4hereford.com/pdf/LSE_Lecture_Burke_and_Oakeshott.pdf.

O'Gorman, Frank. *Edmund Burke: His Political Philosophy*. London: George Allen & Unwin, 1973.

Oh, Irene. *The Rights of God: Islam, Human Rights, and Comparative Ethics*. Washington, D.C.: Georgetown University Press, 2007.

O'Neill, Onora. "The Dark Side of Human Rights." *International Affairs* 81, no. 2 (2005): 427–39.

Paine, Thomas. *Rights of Man: Being an Answer to Mr. Burke's Attack on the French Revolution*. London: J. S. Jordan, 1791.

Price, Richard. *A Discourse on the Love of Our Country*. London: T. Cadell, 1789. Accessed January 15, 2015. http://lf-oll.s3.amazonaws.com/titles/368/1290_Bk.pdf.

Sen, Amartya. "Elements of a Theory of Human Rights." *Philosophy and Public Affairs* 32, no. 4 (2004): 315–56.

Stanlis, Peter J. "The Basis of Burke's Political Conservatism." *Modern Age* 5, no. 3 (1961): 263–74.

Edmund Burke and the Natural Law. Piscataway, NJ: Transaction, 2003.

"Edmund Burke in the Twentieth Century." In *The Relevance of Edmund Burke*, edited by Peter J. Stanlis, 21–58. New York: P.J. Kenedy, 1964.

Turner, Frank M. "Edmund Burke: The Political Actor Thinking." Introduction to Edmund Burke, *Reflections on the Revolution in France*, edited by Frank M. Turner. New Haven, CT: Yale University Press, 2003.

United Nations. Universal Declaration of Human Rights. Accessed January 14, 2015. www.un.org/en/documents/udhr/.

Wollstonecraft, Mary. *A Vindication of the Rights of Men, in a Letter to the Right Honourable Edmund Burke; Occasioned by His Reflections on the Revolution in France*. Charlottesville, VA: Intelex, 2004.

THE MACAT LIBRARY
BY DISCIPLINE

AFRICANA STUDIES

Chinua Achebe's *An Image of Africa: Racism in Conrad's Heart of Darkness*
W. E. B. Du Bois's *The Souls of Black Folk*
Zora Neale Huston's *Characteristics of Negro Expression*
Martin Luther King Jr's *Why We Can't Wait*
Toni Morrison's *Playing in the Dark: Whiteness in the American Literary Imagination*

ANTHROPOLOGY

Arjun Appadurai's *Modernity at Large: Cultural Dimensions of Globalisation*
Philippe Ariès's *Centuries of Childhood*
Franz Boas's *Race, Language and Culture*
Kim Chan & Renée Mauborgne's *Blue Ocean Strategy*
Jared Diamond's *Guns, Germs & Steel: the Fate of Human Societies*
Jared Diamond's *Collapse: How Societies Choose to Fail or Survive*
E. E. Evans-Pritchard's *Witchcraft, Oracles and Magic Among the Azande*
James Ferguson's *The Anti-Politics Machine*
Clifford Geertz's *The Interpretation of Cultures*
David Graeber's *Debt: the First 5000 Years*
Karen Ho's *Liquidated: An Ethnography of Wall Street*
Geert Hofstede's *Culture's Consequences: Comparing Values, Behaviors, Institutes and Organizations across Nations*
Claude Lévi-Strauss's *Structural Anthropology*
Jay Macleod's *Ain't No Makin' It: Aspirations and Attainment in a Low-Income Neighborhood*
Saba Mahmood's *The Politics of Piety: The Islamic Revival and the Feminist Subject*
Marcel Mauss's *The Gift*

BUSINESS

Jean Lave & Etienne Wenger's *Situated Learning*
Theodore Levitt's *Marketing Myopia*
Burton G. Malkiel's *A Random Walk Down Wall Street*
Douglas McGregor's *The Human Side of Enterprise*
Michael Porter's *Competitive Strategy: Creating and Sustaining Superior Performance*
John Kotter's *Leading Change*
C. K. Prahalad & Gary Hamel's *The Core Competence of the Corporation*

CRIMINOLOGY

Michelle Alexander's *The New Jim Crow: Mass Incarceration in the Age of Colorblindness*
Michael R. Gottfredson & Travis Hirschi's *A General Theory of Crime*
Richard Herrnstein & Charles A. Murray's *The Bell Curve: Intelligence and Class Structure in American Life*
Elizabeth Loftus's *Eyewitness Testimony*
Jay Macleod's *Ain't No Makin' It: Aspirations and Attainment in a Low-Income Neighborhood*
Philip Zimbardo's *The Lucifer Effect*

ECONOMICS

Janet Abu-Lughod's *Before European Hegemony*
Ha-Joon Chang's *Kicking Away the Ladder*
David Brion Davis's *The Problem of Slavery in the Age of Revolution*
Milton Friedman's *The Role of Monetary Policy*
Milton Friedman's *Capitalism and Freedom*
David Graeber's *Debt: the First 5000 Years*
Friedrich Hayek's *The Road to Serfdom*
Karen Ho's *Liquidated: An Ethnography of Wall Street*

John Maynard Keynes's *The General Theory of Employment, Interest and Money*
Charles P. Kindleberger's *Manias, Panics and Crashes*
Robert Lucas's *Why Doesn't Capital Flow from Rich to Poor Countries?*
Burton G. Malkiel's *A Random Walk Down Wall Street*
Thomas Robert Malthus's *An Essay on the Principle of Population*
Karl Marx's *Capital*
Thomas Piketty's *Capital in the Twenty-First Century*
Amartya Sen's *Development as Freedom*
Adam Smith's *The Wealth of Nations*
Nassim Nicholas Taleb's *The Black Swan: The Impact of the Highly Improbable*
Amos Tversky's & Daniel Kahneman's *Judgment under Uncertainty: Heuristics and Biases*
Mahbub Ul Haq's *Reflections on Human Development*
Max Weber's *The Protestant Ethic and the Spirit of Capitalism*

FEMINISM AND GENDER STUDIES

Judith Butler's *Gender Trouble*
Simone De Beauvoir's *The Second Sex*
Michel Foucault's *History of Sexuality*
Betty Friedan's *The Feminine Mystique*
Saba Mahmood's *The Politics of Piety: The Islamic Revival and the Feminist Subject*
Joan Wallach Scott's *Gender and the Politics of History*
Mary Wollstonecraft's *A Vindication of the Rights of Woman*
Virginia Woolf's *A Room of One's Own*

GEOGRAPHY

The Brundtland Report's *Our Common Future*
Rachel Carson's *Silent Spring*
Charles Darwin's *On the Origin of Species*
James Ferguson's *The Anti-Politics Machine*
Jane Jacobs's *The Death and Life of Great American Cities*
James Lovelock's *Gaia: A New Look at Life on Earth*
Amartya Sen's *Development as Freedom*
Mathis Wackernagel & William Rees's *Our Ecological Footprint*

HISTORY

Janet Abu-Lughod's *Before European Hegemony*
Benedict Anderson's *Imagined Communities*
Bernard Bailyn's *The Ideological Origins of the American Revolution*
Hanna Batatu's *The Old Social Classes And The Revolutionary Movements Of Iraq*
Christopher Browning's *Ordinary Men: Reserve Police Batallion 101 and the Final Solution in Poland*
Edmund Burke's *Reflections on the Revolution in France*
William Cronon's *Nature's Metropolis: Chicago And The Great West*
Alfred W. Crosby's *The Columbian Exchange*
Hamid Dabashi's *Iran: A People Interrupted*
David Brion Davis's *The Problem of Slavery in the Age of Revolution*
Nathalie Zemon Davis's *The Return of Martin Guerre*
Jared Diamond's *Guns, Germs & Steel: the Fate of Human Societies*
Frank Dikotter's *Mao's Great Famine*
John W Dower's *War Without Mercy: Race And Power In The Pacific War*
W. E. B. Du Bois's *The Souls of Black Folk*
Richard J. Evans's *In Defence of History*
Lucien Febvre's *The Problem of Unbelief in the 16th Century*
Sheila Fitzpatrick's *Everyday Stalinism*

Eric Foner's *Reconstruction: America's Unfinished Revolution, 1863-1877*
Michel Foucault's *Discipline and Punish*
Michel Foucault's *History of Sexuality*
Francis Fukuyama's *The End of History and the Last Man*
John Lewis Gaddis's *We Now Know: Rethinking Cold War History*
Ernest Gellner's *Nations and Nationalism*
Eugene Genovese's *Roll, Jordan, Roll: The World the Slaves Made*
Carlo Ginzburg's *The Night Battles*
Daniel Goldhagen's *Hitler's Willing Executioners*
Jack Goldstone's *Revolution and Rebellion in the Early Modern World*
Antonio Gramsci's *The Prison Notebooks*
Alexander Hamilton, John Jay & James Madison's *The Federalist Papers*
Christopher Hill's *The World Turned Upside Down*
Carole Hillenbrand's *The Crusades: Islamic Perspectives*
Thomas Hobbes's *Leviathan*
Eric Hobsbawm's *The Age Of Revolution*
John A. Hobson's *Imperialism: A Study*
Albert Hourani's *History of the Arab Peoples*
Samuel P. Huntington's *The Clash of Civilizations and the Remaking of World Order*
C. L. R. James's *The Black Jacobins*
Tony Judt's *Postwar: A History of Europe Since 1945*
Ernst Kantorowicz's *The King's Two Bodies: A Study in Medieval Political Theology*
Paul Kennedy's *The Rise and Fall of the Great Powers*
Ian Kershaw's *The "Hitler Myth": Image and Reality in the Third Reich*
John Maynard Keynes's *The General Theory of Employment, Interest and Money*
Charles P. Kindleberger's *Manias, Panics and Crashes*
Martin Luther King Jr's *Why We Can't Wait*
Henry Kissinger's *World Order: Reflections on the Character of Nations and the Course of History*
Thomas Kuhn's *The Structure of Scientific Revolutions*
Georges Lefebvre's *The Coming of the French Revolution*
John Locke's *Two Treatises of Government*
Niccolò Machiavelli's *The Prince*
Thomas Robert Malthus's *An Essay on the Principle of Population*
Mahmood Mamdani's *Citizen and Subject: Contemporary Africa And The Legacy Of Late Colonialism*
Karl Marx's *Capital*
Stanley Milgram's *Obedience to Authority*
John Stuart Mill's *On Liberty*
Thomas Paine's *Common Sense*
Thomas Paine's *Rights of Man*
Geoffrey Parker's *Global Crisis: War, Climate Change and Catastrophe in the Seventeenth Century*
Jonathan Riley-Smith's *The First Crusade and the Idea of Crusading*
Jean-Jacques Rousseau's *The Social Contract*
Joan Wallach Scott's *Gender and the Politics of History*
Theda Skocpol's *States and Social Revolutions*
Adam Smith's *The Wealth of Nations*
Timothy Snyder's *Bloodlands: Europe Between Hitler and Stalin*
Sun Tzu's *The Art of War*
Keith Thomas's *Religion and the Decline of Magic*
Thucydides's *The History of the Peloponnesian War*
Frederick Jackson Turner's *The Significance of the Frontier in American History*
Odd Arne Westad's *The Global Cold War: Third World Interventions And The Making Of Our Times*

The Macat Library By Discipline

LITERATURE

Chinua Achebe's *An Image of Africa: Racism in Conrad's Heart of Darkness*
Roland Barthes's *Mythologies*
Homi K. Bhabha's *The Location of Culture*
Judith Butler's *Gender Trouble*
Simone De Beauvoir's *The Second Sex*
Ferdinand De Saussure's *Course in General Linguistics*
T. S. Eliot's *The Sacred Wood: Essays on Poetry and Criticism*
Zora Neale Huston's *Characteristics of Negro Expression*
Toni Morrison's *Playing in the Dark: Whiteness in the American Literary Imagination*
Edward Said's *Orientalism*
Gayatri Chakravorty Spivak's *Can the Subaltern Speak?*
Mary Wollstonecraft's *A Vindication of the Rights of Women*
Virginia Woolf's *A Room of One's Own*

PHILOSOPHY

Elizabeth Anscombe's *Modern Moral Philosophy*
Hannah Arendt's *The Human Condition*
Aristotle's *Metaphysics*
Aristotle's *Nicomachean Ethics*
Edmund Gettier's *Is Justified True Belief Knowledge?*
Georg Wilhelm Friedrich Hegel's *Phenomenology of Spirit*
David Hume's *Dialogues Concerning Natural Religion*
David Hume's *The Enquiry for Human Understanding*
Immanuel Kant's *Religion within the Boundaries of Mere Reason*
Immanuel Kant's *Critique of Pure Reason*
Søren Kierkegaard's *The Sickness Unto Death*
Søren Kierkegaard's *Fear and Trembling*
C. S. Lewis's *The Abolition of Man*
Alasdair MacIntyre's *After Virtue*
Marcus Aurelius's *Meditations*
Friedrich Nietzsche's *On the Genealogy of Morality*
Friedrich Nietzsche's *Beyond Good and Evil*
Plato's *Republic*
Plato's *Symposium*
Jean-Jacques Rousseau's *The Social Contract*
Gilbert Ryle's *The Concept of Mind*
Baruch Spinoza's *Ethics*
Sun Tzu's *The Art of War*
Ludwig Wittgenstein's *Philosophical Investigations*

POLITICS

Benedict Anderson's *Imagined Communities*
Aristotle's *Politics*
Bernard Bailyn's *The Ideological Origins of the American Revolution*
Edmund Burke's *Reflections on the Revolution in France*
John C. Calhoun's *A Disquisition on Government*
Ha-Joon Chang's *Kicking Away the Ladder*
Hamid Dabashi's *Iran: A People Interrupted*
Hamid Dabashi's *Theology of Discontent: The Ideological Foundation of the Islamic Revolution in Iran*
Robert Dahl's *Democracy and its Critics*
Robert Dahl's *Who Governs?*
David Brion Davis's *The Problem of Slavery in the Age of Revolution*

Alexis De Tocqueville's *Democracy in America*
James Ferguson's *The Anti-Politics Machine*
Frank Dikotter's *Mao's Great Famine*
Sheila Fitzpatrick's *Everyday Stalinism*
Eric Foner's *Reconstruction: America's Unfinished Revolution, 1863-1877*
Milton Friedman's *Capitalism and Freedom*
Francis Fukuyama's *The End of History and the Last Man*
John Lewis Gaddis's *We Now Know: Rethinking Cold War History*
Ernest Gellner's *Nations and Nationalism*
David Graeber's *Debt: the First 5000 Years*
Antonio Gramsci's *The Prison Notebooks*
Alexander Hamilton, John Jay & James Madison's *The Federalist Papers*
Friedrich Hayek's *The Road to Serfdom*
Christopher Hill's *The World Turned Upside Down*
Thomas Hobbes's *Leviathan*
John A. Hobson's *Imperialism: A Study*
Samuel P. Huntington's *The Clash of Civilizations and the Remaking of World Order*
Tony Judt's *Postwar: A History of Europe Since 1945*
David C. Kang's *China Rising: Peace, Power and Order in East Asia*
Paul Kennedy's *The Rise and Fall of Great Powers*
Robert Keohane's *After Hegemony*
Martin Luther King Jr.'s *Why We Can't Wait*
Henry Kissinger's *World Order: Reflections on the Character of Nations and the Course of History*
John Locke's *Two Treatises of Government*
Niccolò Machiavelli's *The Prince*
Thomas Robert Malthus's *An Essay on the Principle of Population*
Mahmood Mamdani's *Citizen and Subject: Contemporary Africa And The Legacy Of
Late Colonialism*
Karl Marx's *Capital*
John Stuart Mill's *On Liberty*
John Stuart Mill's *Utilitarianism*
Hans Morgenthau's *Politics Among Nations*
Thomas Paine's *Common Sense*
Thomas Paine's *Rights of Man*
Thomas Piketty's *Capital in the Twenty-First Century*
Robert D. Putman's *Bowling Alone*
John Rawls's *Theory of Justice*
Jean-Jacques Rousseau's *The Social Contract*
Theda Skocpol's *States and Social Revolutions*
Adam Smith's *The Wealth of Nations*
Sun Tzu's *The Art of War*
Henry David Thoreau's *Civil Disobedience*
Thucydides's *The History of the Peloponnesian War*
Kenneth Waltz's *Theory of International Politics*
Max Weber's *Politics as a Vocation*
Odd Arne Westad's *The Global Cold War: Third World Interventions And The Making Of Our Times*

POSTCOLONIAL STUDIES

Roland Barthes's *Mythologies*
Frantz Fanon's *Black Skin, White Masks*
Homi K. Bhabha's *The Location of Culture*
Gustavo Gutiérrez's *A Theology of Liberation*
Edward Said's *Orientalism*
Gayatri Chakravorty Spivak's *Can the Subaltern Speak?*

The Macat Library By Discipline

PSYCHOLOGY

Gordon Allport's *The Nature of Prejudice*
Alan Baddeley & Graham Hitch's *Aggression: A Social Learning Analysis*
Albert Bandura's *Aggression: A Social Learning Analysis*
Leon Festinger's *A Theory of Cognitive Dissonance*
Sigmund Freud's *The Interpretation of Dreams*
Betty Friedan's *The Feminine Mystique*
Michael R. Gottfredson & Travis Hirschi's *A General Theory of Crime*
Eric Hoffer's *The True Believer: Thoughts on the Nature of Mass Movements*
William James's *Principles of Psychology*
Elizabeth Loftus's *Eyewitness Testimony*
A. H. Maslow's *A Theory of Human Motivation*
Stanley Milgram's *Obedience to Authority*
Steven Pinker's *The Better Angels of Our Nature*
Oliver Sacks's *The Man Who Mistook His Wife For a Hat*
Richard Thaler & Cass Sunstein's *Nudge: Improving Decisions About Health, Wealth and Happiness*
Amos Tversky's *Judgment under Uncertainty: Heuristics and Biases*
Philip Zimbardo's *The Lucifer Effect*

SCIENCE

Rachel Carson's *Silent Spring*
William Cronon's *Nature's Metropolis: Chicago And The Great West*
Alfred W. Crosby's *The Columbian Exchange*
Charles Darwin's *On the Origin of Species*
Richard Dawkin's *The Selfish Gene*
Thomas Kuhn's *The Structure of Scientific Revolutions*
Geoffrey Parker's *Global Crisis: War, Climate Change and Catastrophe in the Seventeenth Century*
Mathis Wackernagel & William Rees's *Our Ecological Footprint*

SOCIOLOGY

Michelle Alexander's *The New Jim Crow: Mass Incarceration in the Age of Colorblindness*
Gordon Allport's *The Nature of Prejudice*
Albert Bandura's *Aggression: A Social Learning Analysis*
Hanna Batatu's *The Old Social Classes And The Revolutionary Movements Of Iraq*
Ha-Joon Chang's *Kicking Away the Ladder*
W. E. B. Du Bois's *The Souls of Black Folk*
Émile Durkheim's *On Suicide*
Frantz Fanon's *Black Skin, White Masks*
Frantz Fanon's *The Wretched of the Earth*
Eric Foner's *Reconstruction: America's Unfinished Revolution, 1863-1877*
Eugene Genovese's *Roll, Jordan, Roll: The World the Slaves Made*
Jack Goldstone's *Revolution and Rebellion in the Early Modern World*
Antonio Gramsci's *The Prison Notebooks*
Richard Herrnstein & Charles A Murray's *The Bell Curve: Intelligence and Class Structure in American Life*
Eric Hoffer's *The True Believer: Thoughts on the Nature of Mass Movements*
Jane Jacobs's *The Death and Life of Great American Cities*
Robert Lucas's *Why Doesn't Capital Flow from Rich to Poor Countries?*
Jay Macleod's *Ain't No Makin' It: Aspirations and Attainment in a Low Income Neighborhood*
Elaine May's *Homeward Bound: American Families in the Cold War Era*
Douglas McGregor's *The Human Side of Enterprise*
C. Wright Mills's *The Sociological Imagination*

Thomas Piketty's *Capital in the Twenty-First Century*
Robert D. Putman's *Bowling Alone*
David Riesman's *The Lonely Crowd: A Study of the Changing American Character*
Edward Said's *Orientalism*
Joan Wallach Scott's *Gender and the Politics of History*
Theda Skocpol's *States and Social Revolutions*
Max Weber's *The Protestant Ethic and the Spirit of Capitalism*

THEOLOGY

Augustine's *Confessions*
Benedict's *Rule of St Benedict*
Gustavo Gutiérrez's *A Theology of Liberation*
Carole Hillenbrand's *The Crusades: Islamic Perspectives*
David Hume's *Dialogues Concerning Natural Religion*
Immanuel Kant's *Religion within the Boundaries of Mere Reason*
Ernst Kantorowicz's *The King's Two Bodies: A Study in Medieval Political Theology*
Søren Kierkegaard's *The Sickness Unto Death*
C. S. Lewis's *The Abolition of Man*
Saba Mahmood's *The Politics of Piety: The Islamic Revival and the Feminist Subject*
Baruch Spinoza's *Ethics*
Keith Thomas's *Religion and the Decline of Magic*

COMING SOON

Chris Argyris's *The Individual and the Organisation*
Seyla Benhabib's *The Rights of Others*
Walter Benjamin's *The Work Of Art in the Age of Mechanical Reproduction*
John Berger's *Ways of Seeing*
Pierre Bourdieu's *Outline of a Theory of Practice*
Mary Douglas's *Purity and Danger*
Roland Dworkin's *Taking Rights Seriously*
James G. March's *Exploration and Exploitation in Organisational Learning*
Ikujiro Nonaka's *A Dynamic Theory of Organizational Knowledge Creation*
Griselda Pollock's *Vision and Difference*
Amartya Sen's *Inequality Re-Examined*
Susan Sontag's *On Photography*
Yasser Tabbaa's *The Transformation of Islamic Art*
Ludwig von Mises's *Theory of Money and Credit*

Macat Disciplines

Access the greatest ideas and thinkers across entire disciplines, including

CRIMINOLOGY

Michelle Alexander's
The New Jim Crow: Mass Incarceration in the Age of Colorblindness

Michael R. Gottfredson & Travis Hirschi's
A General Theory of Crime

Elizabeth Loftus's
Eyewitness Testimony

Richard Herrnstein & Charles A. Murray's
The Bell Curve: Intelligence and Class Structure in American Life

Jay Macleod's
Ain't No Makin' It: Aspirations and Attainment in a Low-Income Neighborhood

Philip Zimbardo's
The Lucifer Effect

Macat Disciplines

Access the greatest ideas and thinkers across entire disciplines, including

INEQUALITY

Ha-Joon Chang's, *Kicking Away the Ladder*

David Graeber's, *Debt: The First 5000 Years*

Robert E. Lucas's, *Why Doesn't Capital Flow from Rich To Poor Countries?*

Thomas Piketty's, *Capital in the Twenty-First Century*

Amartya Sen's, *Inequality Re-Examined*

Mahbub Ul Haq's, *Reflections on Human Development*

Macat analyses are available from all good bookshops and libraries.

Access hundreds of analyses through one, multimedia tool.

Join free for one month **library.macat.com**

Macat Disciplines

Access the greatest ideas and thinkers across entire disciplines, including

MAN AND THE ENVIRONMENT

The Brundtland Report's, *Our Common Future*
Rachel Carson's, *Silent Spring*
James Lovelock's, *Gaia: A New Look at Life on Earth*
Mathis Wackernagel & William Rees's, *Our Ecological Footprint*

Macat analyses are available from all good bookshops and libraries.

Access hundreds of analyses through one, multimedia tool.

Join free for one month **library.macat.com**

Macat Pairs

Analyse historical and modern issues
from opposite sides of an argument.
Pairs include:

RACE AND IDENTITY

Zora Neale Hurston's
Characteristics of Negro Expression

Using material collected on anthropological expeditions to the South, Zora Neale Hurston explains how expression in African American culture in the early twentieth century departs from the art of white America. At the time, African American art was often criticized for copying white culture. For Hurston, this criticism misunderstood how art works. European tradition views art as something fixed. But Hurston describes a creative process that is alive, ever-changing, and largely improvisational. She maintains that African American art works through a process called 'mimicry'—where an imitated object or verbal pattern, for example, is reshaped and altered until it becomes something new, novel—and worthy of attention.

Frantz Fanon's
Black Skin, White Masks

Black Skin, White Masks offers a radical analysis of the psychological effects of colonization on the colonized.

Fanon witnessed the effects of colonization first hand both in his birthplace, Martinique, and again later in life when he worked as a psychiatrist in another French colony, Algeria. His text is uncompromising in form and argument. He dissects the dehumanizing effects of colonialism, arguing that it destroys the native sense of identity, forcing people to adapt to an alien set of values—including a core belief that they are inferior. This results in deep psychological trauma.

Fanon's work played a pivotal role in the civil rights movements of the 1960s.

Macat analyses are available from all good bookshops and libraries.

Access hundreds of analyses through one, multimedia tool.
Join free for one month **library.macat.com**

Macat Pairs

Analyse historical and modern issues from opposite sides of an argument. Pairs include:

INTERNATIONAL RELATIONS IN THE 21ST CENTURY

Samuel P. Huntington's
The Clash of Civilisations

In his highly influential 1996 book, Huntington offers a vision of a post-Cold War world in which conflict takes place not between competing ideologies but between cultures. The worst clash, he argues, will be between the Islamic world and the West: the West's arrogance and belief that its culture is a "gift" to the world will come into conflict with Islam's obstinacy and concern that its culture is under attack from a morally decadent "other."

Clash inspired much debate between different political schools of thought. But its greatest impact came in helping define American foreign policy in the wake of the 2001 terrorist attacks in New York and Washington.

Francis Fukuyama's
The End of History and the Last Man

Published in 1992, *The End of History and the Last Man* argues that capitalist democracy is the final destination for all societies. Fukuyama believed democracy triumphed during the Cold War because it lacks the "fundamental contradictions" inherent in communism and satisfies our yearning for freedom and equality. Democracy therefore marks the endpoint in the evolution of ideology, and so the "end of history." There will still be "events," but no fundamental change in ideology.

Macat Pairs

*Analyse historical and modern issues
from opposite sides of an argument.
Pairs include:*

HOW TO RUN AN ECONOMY

John Maynard Keynes's
*The General Theory OF Employment,
Interest and Money*

Classical economics suggests that market economies
are self-correcting in times of recession or depression,
and tend toward full employment and output. But
English economist John Maynard Keynes disagrees.

In his ground-breaking 1936 study *The General
Theory*, Keynes argues that traditional economics
has misunderstood the causes of unemployment.
Employment is not determined by the price of labor;
it is directly linked to demand. Keynes believes market
economies are by nature unstable, and so require
government intervention. Spurred on by the social
catastrophe of the Great Depression of the 1930s,
he sets out to revolutionize the way the world thinks

Milton Friedman's
The Role of Monetary Policy

Friedman's 1968 paper changed the course of
economic theory. In just 17 pages, he demolished
existing theory and outlined an effective alternate
monetary policy designed to secure 'high employment,
stable prices and rapid growth.'

Friedman demonstrated that monetary policy plays
a vital role in broader economic stability and argued
that economists got their monetary policy wrong
in the 1950s and 1960s by misunderstanding the
relationship between inflation and unemployment.
Previous generations of economists had believed
that governments could permanently decrease
unemployment by permitting inflation—and vice versa.
Friedman's most original contribution was to show that
this supposed trade-off is an illusion that only works in
the short term.

Macat analyses are available from all good bookshops and libraries.

Access hundreds of analyses through one, multimedia tool.
Join free for one month **library.macat.com**

Printed in the United States
by Baker & Taylor Publisher Services